Simulation Games

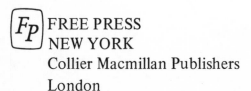

An Introduction
for the
Social Studies Teacher

Samuel A. Livingston and Clarice Stasz Stoll

Fp FREE PRESS
NEW YORK
Collier Macmillan Publishers
London

This book is dedicated to social studies teachers and to their students.

The Free Press
A Division of Macmillan Publishing Co., Inc.

Collier Macmillan Canada Ltd.

Library of Congress Catalog Card Number: 77-171567

printing number
1 2 3 4 5 6 7 8 9 10

Table
of
Contents

Preface

We have written this book for social studies teachers who are unfamiliar or inexperienced with the technique of teaching by means of simulation games. After reading Chapter 1, you should know what a simulation is, how simulation for teaching differs from simulation for training, and how a simulation game differs from a role-playing exercise or a "didactic unit." Chapter 1 also contains descriptions of four commercially available simulation games, to show the similarities and differences among simulation games.

Chapter 2 presents a comparison of simulation games with other educational media and illustrates the ways in which simulation games accomplish some common social studies objectives: knowledge of terms and concepts, knowledge of facts, knowledge of structures and relationships, decision-making skills, interpersonal skills, and development of mature attitudes.

Chapters 3 and 4 are "How to do it" chapters. After reading Chapter 3, you should be able to do all of the following things:

(1) select a suitable simulation game for your class, without having seen the game played beforehand;
(2) administer a simulation game in class with confidence;
(3) conduct a class discussion that will help the students learn as much as possible from a simulation game; and
(4) construct tests and questionnaires to find out how much your students have learned from a simulation game.

After reading Chapter 4, you should be able to design an original simulation game that will be realistic, playable, and effective as a teaching device. Of course, the same techniques which are used in designing an original game can also be used to modify an existing game.

Chapter 5 presents our answer to the question: "How well do simulation games actually accomplish the objectives for which they are designed?" For each of several claims commonly made for simulation games (including some that we make in the first four chapters), we present a summary of the relevant research that has been reported.

We hope that you will find this book readable, enjoyable, and, above all, useful.

We are indebted to a number of others for their help in completing this book. Irving Naiburg, our editor, was a major source of encouragement and provided many helpful suggestions. William Coplin, Stephen Ellenwood, Gail Fennessey, Lynn Mayer, Paul MacFarlane, Charles Roberts, and Christine Schulze all read early drafts and reacted with valuable comments, criticisms, and suggestions. Finally, we thank Phyllis Wilson and David Wirtz for their competent and efficient assistance in the preparation of the manuscript.

SAMUEL A. LIVINGSTON
CLARICE STASZ STOLL

1 Introduction to Simulation

WHAT IS A SIMULATION GAME?

Simulation and gaming include several types of classroom activities that share a common base. A *simulation* is a working model of an object or situation. For example, during space flights, the television networks often show simulations of the maneuvers of the space ships because it is not possible to televise the actual maneuvers. A *social simulation* is a representation of a situation involving human interaction. *Games* are activities with goals and rules. A *simulation game* is a game that is also a simulation—that is, a game that is intended to represent some other situation. An *instructional game* is any game intended for teaching a subject or skill. (Games have been devised to teach such diverse subjects as mathematics, spelling, history, and business decision-making.)

This book is about the use and design of *instructional social simulation games*. Hundreds of such games are available for use in social studies classrooms today.[1] Although many of the older games were designed for junior or senior high school courses, there are now simulation games for elementary grades, college and graduate school courses, and adult education as well. Regardless of the content of the course, the ability and interests of the students, and the time and space available, you are likely to find at least one, and perhaps several, suitable simulation games. The following descriptions should give you a better idea of what a simulation game is, and why the technique has special value for the social studies.[2]

FOUR EXAMPLES

Life Career

Life Career was one of the first social simulation games and remains one of the most ambitious in the amount of information it incorporates. It simulates the labor market, educational opportuni-

ties, marriage, and leisure in the United States. The game represents eight years in the life of a fictitious person for whom the players must make decisions. The players' folder instructs as follows:

Each round of *Life Career* represents one year in this person's life. You must decide how he will spend his time each year. For each round, your team must figure out your person's family budget and must decide if your person:

1. is going to stay in school this year;
2. wants to have a job this year;
3. wants to get married or have a child this year, and how much time he will spend with his family;
4. is going to have any leisure activities.

The major purpose of *Life Career* is to inform students about career decision-making in our society. The game accomplishes this in two ways. First, it gives the student a feeling for the future by showing how present-day decisions can have lasting consequences. Second, it provides a wide range of information about available career opportunities.

The game is structured so that teams of three or four players compete with one another to provide the "most successful life" for the same fictional person. Each team receives a profile which describes the fictional person's family life, his academic abilities, his recreational interests, and his financial situation. See the sample profile for "Anne" as an example.

The players then complete a time schedule form showing how many hours Anne will spend at each activity—school, study, work, family, sports, and so forth—in a typical week of the year. The players must make many decisions in order to complete the form. If Anne attends school, every course in her program of study must be selected by name. If the players decide that Anne should enter a trade school or college, they must fill out an application form. (Of course, Anne must meet the entrance requirements listed in the school catalog.) If they decide that Anne should get a job, they must look through simulated want ads that describe the jobs available at that point in the game. A job catalog lists approximately 100 occupations, from unskilled through professional, providing such information as starting salary, projected

[1] See the comprehensive listing and descriptions of these games in Zuckerman and Horn (1973). (*Note:* Throughout *Simulation Games*, full bibliographical data are found at the conclusion of each chapter.)

[2] The appendix to this volume contains a list of names and addresses of some of the publishers of simulation games.

1

SAMPLE PROFILE

ANNE

Anne is almost 17 years old, although she is just starting her junior year. She had to repeat a year in grammar school, and even so she has just barely managed to be promoted each year. Her verbal and quantitative skills are below average, and she has never done well in English, social studies, languages, math, science, and other academic subjects. She has scored average in vocational skills tests, however, and she works well with her hands.

Anne hates school and has gotten so used to be being behind the other students in her classes that she has given up trying. Since her evenings are spent with her boy friend or at her part-time job clerking in a dime store, she rarely has her homework done and is always in trouble with her teachers. She is absent a lot, and the truant officer has warned her mother that she may get into real trouble if her attendance record does not improve. She also got into trouble last year when she and two other girls were caught smoking in the school building during lunch hour.

Anne's boy friend is 18 and has a job as a factory assembler. He earned $3500 last year and has his own car. He wants to marry Anne and has promised to take her to New York for a honeymoon. He finished three years of high school and doesn't think it is im-portant for Anne to graduate.

Anne lives with her mother and younger sister. Her father deserted the family when she was quite young, and her mother supports the family on what she earns as a waitress and maid (usually about $3000 a year). She wants Anne to stay in school and get enough education to get a decent job. She is anxious for her daughter not to repeat her own mistakes and thinks she is too young to marry.

But Anne wants to get away from the unhappiness of her home and to have a chance to enjoy life. She figures that if she worked full-time, she and her boy friend would have enough to get married and start saving for a house of their own.

Although she likes excitement and would like to travel, Anne's greatest ambition is to have a home of her own. She has always helped her mother with the housework and is an excellent cook. The one time she really shone in school was in a 7th grade home economics course, where she learned to use a sewing machine and made some curtains for home and some simple clothes for herself. The teacher was impressed by Anne's ability to work with her hands and felt that she showed a flair for design.

ANNE'S ABILITIES

Verbal — below average
Quantitative — below average
Vocational — average

ANNE'S GRADE TRANSCRIPT

High School Freshman		High School Sophomore	
Course Taken	Grades	Course Taken	Grades
English	D	English	F
Social Studies	D	Social Studies	D
Science	F	Science	D
Math	C	Commercial	C
Phys. Ed.	Pass	Home Ec.	C
		Phys. Ed.	Pass

Minimum Income Required For First Round = $3000

SOURCE: Sarane S. Boocock, *Life Career*. Published by Western Publishing Co., New York, 1969. Developed by Academic Games Associates, Inc.; © 1968, 1969, by Sarane S. Boocock.

---

demand for workers, and the proportion of male and female workers. If Anne meets the requirements for a job, one of the players spins a spinner to see if she gets it. The spinner is divided into ten sectors, labeled as follows:

"Congratulations, you get the job."
"Sorry, you didn't get the job."
"Yes, if there are 500,000 workers or more in this field."
"Yes, if your last two years' grade average was C or better."
"Yes, if your last two years' grade average was B or better."
"Yes, if there is a growing demand for workers in this field."
"Yes, if 75 per cent or more of the workers in this field are the same sex as you."
"Yes, if you have held the same or similar job before."
"Yes, if you have special abilities for this job."
"Yes, if you have held a job before."

The first two sectors each occupy 22 per cent of the spinner; the other eight occupy 7 per cent each.

Spinners like this one make students aware of some of the things which influence "chance" events in their lives. Another spinner determines

Anne's marriage prospects; it tells the age and occupation of each potential spouse. This spinner shows the players that their own age and educational achievement will partially determine some of the qualities of the persons who may be interested in them as husbands or wives.

Once the players have made all the required decisions for a year of Anne's life, their score is calculated. The scoring system is based upon a wide range of data, including census information, labor statistics, educational research, and sociological studies of leisure. Although the system is complex, scores are not difficult to calculate, because there are a number of tables to assist the scorer. The team's score for the round is the sum of four separate subscores:

1. *Education.* This score is determined by the grades Anne gets and by her ability; high grades mean more to a student of less ability. Anne's grades, in turn, are determined by her ability, by the amount of time she studies, and by chance.
2. *Occupation.* For a part-time job, the number of points depends upon the person's economic situation. Since Anne's family is poor, a part-time job for her is worth two points per hour, in contrast to one-half point per hour for a person with no financial problems. For full-time jobs, the number of points changes with the length of time on the job and the skill category of the job. Unskilled jobs decrease in value over the years, while professional or highly skilled jobs increase in value.
3. *Family.* Points for helping at home depend upon the person's family situation. Anne does not get along with her parents, so she earns fewer points for time spent helping at home. If she marries, her family score will depend partly upon her education, the number of years she has been married, and her husband's economic situation.
4. *Leisure.* The number of points for these activities depends on the variety of activities chosen and the degree to which they match the person's interests. Since Anne is very sociable, "fun with friends" is worth more to her than solitary activities.

From this description it should be clear that the scores are somewhat individualized, in that they depend on Anne's personal characteristics. If the students play the game again with a different profile, the rewards for some of the activities will be different. The students can then see that activities that make for a rewarding life for one person may not be rewarding for another.

Teachers sometimes comment that *Life Career* excludes certain important career opportunities that are available in our society. For example, the players cannot have their fictional person go into business for himself or seek a career as a professional entertainer or athlete. Also, the choice of artistic occupations in the game is extremely limited. This is a valid criticism, and we shall show later how the "faults" that make a game an imperfect simulation can become the basis for an educationally valuable discussion.

SIMSOC

SIMSOC (Simulated Society) is a game very different from *Life Career.* Designed for introductory social science, sociology, or political science classes in senior high school or college, *SIMSOC* is much less programmed than *Life Career.* Its purpose is to confront students with problems relating to power, authority, trust, and leadership.

Between twenty and sixty students can play in one simulated society. Each player is a citizen in the society, and may seek affiliation with one of seven groups: basic industry, innovative industry, two political parties, an employee interest group, mass media, or judicial council. Each group is assigned specific aims in the society, which it will attempt to achieve with the resources it has.

There are four regions in the game, represented by four rooms or partitioned areas. Players cannot move from one region to another without travel tickets, which cost money (Simbucks).

Each player earns an income (in Simbucks) from his group and must use the income toward subsistence. If he cannot provide for himself over two rounds, he "dies" and leaves the game (to assist the administrator).

Players choose their own personal goals in *SIMSOC* from the following three:

1. *Power.* I will try to influence what happens in the society as much as possible.
2. *Wealth.* I will try to accumulate as many Simbucks as possible at the end of the game.
3. *Popularity.* I will try to become as well liked by other members of *SIMSOC* as I possibly can.

These choices are not used to pick a winner, for there are no winners in *SIMSOC.* Their purpose is to help the player form a general orientation to the game.[3] It is the state of the society as a whole that determines the success of the players. A variety of "national indicators" are calculated at the end of each session as a means of measuring the general "health" of the society:

Food and Energy Surplus: This indicator represents how well the society is adapting to its physical environment. Is it developing its resources to meet the needs of

---

[3] In the second edition of *SIMSOC,* these personal goals are changed somewhat. "Style of life" has been substituted for "wealth," and "center of attention" has been substituted for "popularity." "Security" has been added as a fourth possibility, and the player has been given the option of stating a personal goal not among those suggested.

its population? Is it replenishing those resources that it consumes? A higher score means an abundant food and energy supply.

Standard of Living. This represents the consumption level of the society. How well are the citizens of the society living at the present time? A higher score means a higher standard of living.

Social Cohesion. This represents how well different groups of citizens are integrated. Are there destructive conflicts between groups?

Public Commitment. This represents the degree of commitment by citizens of the society to its social structure and values. Are there large numbers of alienated citizens who feel estranged from the society and who do not participate in it in a constructive way? The higher the score on public commitment, the less the degree of alienation among the citizens.

These indicators are affected by the number of "dead" and unemployed in the society and by the economic decisions of the industry groups. However, players can also decide to invest their money in two types of public programs: research-and-conservation or welfare services. These investments improve the national indicators.

Actual play is not highly structured. Players may operate with or without a government, and any type of government is permissible. Any person or group can create a police force with wide powers of arrest. None of the groups are told exactly what to do to achieve their aims. There is no right or wrong way to play the game. The object is to deal with the many decisions and problems. The game ends whenever one of the national indicators falls below zero. This means that the players have not been successful in some area—for example, in meeting the food and energy needs of the society.

SIMSOC requires about ten hours of play, which may be in fifty-minute sessions spread over a period of weeks or concentrated into a few days. The game works best when a separate room is used for each of the four regions. Although these requirements are not absolute, they illustrate the amount of time and the facilities that some games require for maximum effectiveness.

Diplomacy

Diplomacy is a simulation game designed primarily for entertainment rather than instruction. Yet it has educational value and can be used effectively in a social studies, history, or political science class. The game simulates the international situation of Europe in 1900. The seven players represent the major powers: England, France, Germany, Russia, Austria-Hungary, Italy, and Turkey. Each player's goal is to control as much of Europe as possible. Thus a player can achieve his

goal only at the expense of some other player or players. This feature—direct, "zero-sum" competition—distinguishes *Diplomacy* from both *SIMSOC* and *Life Career.*

Control over territory is established by military force. Each of the great powers of Europe is divided into five, six, or seven provinces, while each of the smaller independent countries comprises a single province. A number of these provinces, including several of the independent countries, are designated as "supply centers." For each supply center that a player controls, he can maintain one army or fleet. The player directs his armies and fleets by means of secret written orders; when all players have finished writing their orders, the orders are read and any resulting conflicts are resolved in favor of the stronger force. After every second move, the number of armies and fleets at each player's command is adjusted to the number of supply centers he controls.

Between moves, the players are given time to negotiate agreements and alliances. However, the rules of the game do not prevent any player from violating these agreements or even from making conflicting agreements. Thus, like real heads of state, the players may keep agreements only as long as they believe it is in their interest to do so.

All simulation games present a simplified view of reality, and *Diplomacy* is no exception. However, because *Diplomacy* is intended primarily for entertainment, it contains certain deliberate distortions of reality. The most obvious of these is the relative power of the major countries at the start of the game; they have been made as nearly equal in power as possible. The rules governing movement reflect another distortion: an army can march from Norway to the Crimea in the same length of time as from Berlin to Vienna.

In spite of these distortions, *Diplomacy* is a valuable educational tool as well as an absorbing game. It can arouse students' interest in a study of the international politics of nineteenth-century Europe. It also illustrates the influence of geography on foreign policy. But perhaps its greatest value lies in its ability to confront the player with the central problem facing foreign policy makers throughout history: the defense of a country surrounded by potentially hostile neighbors. No player in *Diplomacy* can stand alone against the rest and survive. No matter how skillfully he uses his forces, he can be crushed by a powerful opposing coalition. Skillful diplomacy is necessary for survival. Thus, *Diplomacy* is not primarily a game about war, but a game about international agreements. As such, it can offer an insight into the thinking of real national leaders, not only in 1900, but at other times in history as well.

The Road Game

The Road Game is a good example of a simulation game for younger students. Designed for fifth or sixth graders, the game requires no reading or calculations on the part of the student. Its purpose is to lead the students to examine human behavior in situations where power or status is at issue and to consider the purpose of rules in society. The class is divided into four teams, each identified by a color. A large sheet of paper placed on the floor is divided into four equal areas, with each team assigned ownership of one area. Each team also receives one paintbrush and a pot of paint in the team's identifying color.

The teacher begins the game by reading a set of fifteen rules. The stated goal for each team is to draw the greatest number of roads from its own area through other areas to the edge of the paper. Other rules specify such things as "neatness counts" or "the team leader cannot be the team painter." As little opportunity for rule clarification is allowed, the players are often uncertain about the details. The teacher refuses to answer questions and tells the students to play the game without referring to him for interpretation of the rules. Typically, as the game proceeds, a number of rules are broken.

Eventually the teacher stops this activity and counts the roads in such a way as to encourage disputes. The next phase of the game is the settling of these disputes. If one team challenges another team's count, the members of the remaining two teams listen to the arguments and vote to determine the outcome by majority rule. Often votes are motivated by self-interest or spite, and in many games, the team with the most roads on the board will find its count reduced to zero, even though it followed the rules as stated by the teacher.

As with most simulation games, the value of this experience depends on the discussion that follows it. The teacher's manual is designed to guide the teacher in leading students to analyze their own behavior during the game. For example, the teacher can ask the students which rules they have ignored and why. Though very simple in design, *The Road Game* frequently stimulates a sophisticated discussion of human behavior. As a result, it can be used with players of almost any age level, including adults. With older students, the teacher should change only the post-game discussion.

There is one potential problem with *The Road Game* that may also be encountered in other games. The game may trigger intense feelings in the players, and arguments may lead to expressions of personal hostility. We emphasize that this is only a potential problem; a skillful and sensitive teacher can prevent these harmful outbursts. Of course, there are times when anger is unavoidable, and the teacher must make a special effort to resolve any ill feelings once the game is completed. Therefore, even though teachers are seldom active participants in their students' games, they must be astute observers.

CHARACTERISTICS OF SIMULATION GAMES

One feature of simulation games that these examples illustrate is the element of *roles:* The players take the roles of decision-makers. This feature often leads people to confuse simulation games with role-playing exercises. The distinction is an important one for anybody who is seriously considering using either a simulation game or a role-playing exercise to achieve a particular instructional objective.

The main difference between a simulation game and a role-playing exercise is in the incentives used to motivate the player. In a simulation game, the scoring system provides rewards which depend on the results of the players' decisions. These results and the accompanying rewards are made to correspond as closely as possible to those in the real situation. In a role-playing exercise the player is simply instructed to act as he thinks the person whose role he is playing would act.

A second difference is in the function of the rules. Role-playing exercises often have rules to forbid players from doing things that people in the real situation could do but seldom or never actually do. In a simulation game these same actions would probably be discouraged by the rewards and penalties of the scoring system. In general, the rules of a simulation game forbid only those actions that would be impossible in the real situation. Actions that are merely unwise or unrealistic are discouraged by their consequences, just as in real life.

Simulation games teach some things which role-playing exercises do not. If you want your students to learn the cause-and-effect relationships that operate in an actual social system, a simulation game will do the job; a role-playing exercise will not. On the other hand, if your objective is to provide students with an insight into their behavior and the behavior of others, a role-playing exercise may be adequate.

A role-playing exercise is much easier to design than a simulation game. The designer of a simulation game must program into the game the consequences of each possible combination of players' decisions. He must realistically represent the resources each person has available in the real situation and the value to each person of each possible outcome. The designer of a role-playing exercise need only write descriptions of each role, state each player's objectives in general terms, and add a few rules to prohibit grossly unrealistic behavior.

Unfortunately for the simulation game user, many firms marketing educational materials (and many individuals who create them) do not recognize the important distinction between simulation games and role-playing exercises. It is possible to order something advertised as a simulation game only to find that you have bought the materials for a role-playing exercise. Catalog descriptions can be misleading; the best way to tell a simulation game from a role-playing exercise is to look at the players' instructions in the light of the distinctions just drawn.

A point which our examples only begin to show is that social simulation games cover a wide range of topics. Like *Diplomacy*, they may simulate a specific historical era, or like *SIMSOC*, they may simulate a more general social system. Games can simulate interactions among nations (*Diplomacy*), among individuals (*SIMSOC*), or between individuals and organizations (*Life Career*).

Another point our examples illustrate is that simulation games have two general instructional purposes: to increase the student's *ability* to *perform* in the real situation and to increase his *knowledge and understanding* of the situation. *Life Career* was designed primarily for training the student in decision-making and career planning. *SIMSOC* was designed to teach social studies concepts and to help the players understand the problems of social organization. It is unlikely that many students will take the same roles in real life that they take in *SIMSOC*, but the students who play *Life Career* will all have to make their own decisions about careers, marriage, and leisure.

Before examining the issue of what a simulation game can do in your classroom, it is worth noting some special cases that fall within the province of our discussion. First, some genuine simulation games do not use the word *game* in their title. (*Life Career* and *SIMSOC* are examples.) Designers often wish to prevent students (and teachers) from misconstruing the seriousness of the activity and to deemphasize winning as the goal of the activity. Nevertheless, these simulations have roles, resources, goals, and rules; hence, in the technical sense, they are games.

There are also some curriculum units that combine simulation, game-like activities, and more conventional school activities such as outside research, book reports, and quizzes. These are sometimes referred to as *didactic units.* In these units, a student's grade for the unit depends partly on his success in the simulation, while the resources available to him in the simulation (for example, money or "influence points") depend on his performance in tests and assignments that are not part of the simulation. Unlike these didactic units, most simulations do *not* integrate test results or course grades with the game, because their designers believe that this feature reduces the motivational impact of the game. They argue that a unique feature of the simulation game is its separation from the competitive framework of classroom grading.[4]

[4] More about this in Chapter 3. See also Stoll (1970).

REFERENCES

Stoll, Clarice S. 1970. "Games Students Play." *Media and Methods*, October, pp. 37-41.

Zuckerman, David W., and Horn, Robert E., 1970. *The Guide to Simulations/Games for Education and Training.* Cambridge, Mass.: Information Resources.

2 Simulation Games as a Medium of Instruction

SUBJECT INFORMATION AND STUDENT PARTICIPATION

Simulation games are different from ordinary classroom experiences in several respects. Table 1 displays some of the characteristics of five media for classroom instruction: textbooks, workbooks, lectures, audio-visual presentations, and simulation games. Class discussion is not included in this table because class discussions are usually based on students' previous experience in some other kind of activity; in fact, any of the activities in the table can serve as the basis for a class discussion.

Of the five media listed in the table, a simulation game is the only medium that both requires an active response from each student and responds to the student's actions. A workbook requires an active response, but most workbooks do not alter their presentation of tasks or information according to the student's responses. A skillful lecturer speaking to an audience of typical class size (25 to 40 students) may alter his presentation according to the students' reactions, but he cannot require active responses from each student. Therefore, simulation games are unlike any other medium of instruction that can be used in a classroom situation. In the interaction they require between the student and the medium, they resemble both the most complex computer-based instructional systems and the kind of instruction that takes place when a teacher works with a very small group of students.

With regard to the number of ways in which information is presented, simulation games take second place only to audio-visual presentations; they do not provide the actual sights and sounds of the real situation. They do provide information through speech, print, pictures, charts, maps, and diagrams. In addition, games often present information by means of the physical position of tokens on a board, the furniture in the room, or even the players themselves.

Perhaps the key characteristic of games for teaching is their ability to motivate students. The teacher does not have to hold up some external source of reward, such as a grade, in order to interest the students in the activity. Games are fun, partly because they have an element of surprise and partly because they give rise to joking and banter among the players. The element of competition makes them exciting. They present the challenge of confronting difficult or confusing or risky situations. They offer the satisfaction of receiving a good score and the opportunity to improve a poor score at the next attempt.

Everyone has played games and, judging by the sales of adult games, most people continue to enjoy them after childhood. By definition, games are not serious activities; that is, once the game is over, winning or losing is not supposed to count

TABLE 1. A COMPARISON OF FIVE INSTRUCTIONAL MEDIA.

	Textbooks	Workbooks	Lectures	Audio-visual presentations	Simulation games
Responsiveness:					
Student must respond actively to medium.	No	Yes	No	No	Yes
Medium responds to student.	No	No	?	No	Yes
Variety of input mode:					
Printed symbols	Yes	Yes	No	Yes	Yes
Pictorial	Yes	Yes	No	Yes	Yes
Spoken language	No	No	Yes	Yes	Yes
Sound effects (not speech)	No	No	No	Yes	No

for much. Hence, people can take more risks in games than in real life. Failure in the game will not result in a lost job, a low course grade, or a loss of friends. Instructional simulation games make use of the fact that the situation is "not serious," even while they give the player important information and practice in making decisions that have serious consequences in real life.[1]

For example, in *Life Career* the player must fill out job-application forms. If he fills out the forms incorrectly, he will suffer only in the game. If his first confrontation with a job application had been in real life, his inexperience in filling out forms might have cost him a job. For another example, in *SIMSOC* a group of players might choose to withhold their labor from the economy and observe the effects of their decision on the social system. In real life, such a decision might have drastic consequences for the individuals who refused to participate, but in the game the players can afford to indulge their curiosity.

It is this special sort of limited responsibility that makes simulation games effective for both training and teaching. The player must experience the consequences of his decisions within the context of the game. The rewards or penalties do not carry over into real life, but the experience the player gains does carry over.

SIMULATION GAMES AND THE SOCIAL STRUCTURE OF THE CLASSROOM

Another characteristic of many simulation games is that they allow students to work together toward their goals. Simulation games frequently incorporate teamwork or encourage cooperative strategies. This contrasts with the usual situation in the American classroom, where competition pits each student against the others.[2] Even simulation games based on individual competition encourage students to learn from each other. The less successful players can observe the strategies of the more successful players and adjust their own strategies accordingly.

Simulation games do more than provide a situation in which students may help each other to learn. They may also cause students to look at each other in new ways. Simulations may require many types of skills that are often overlooked in the usual classroom, such as speechmaking, persuasive talking, and strategic planning. Even students who are poor at regular classroom work involving

reading and writing may be outstanding in simulation games.

Most simulations also affect the student-teacher relationship. The teacher is no longer a judge of student performance. The scoring system does the judging, impartially and automatically. The teacher serves as an interpreter and observer, explaining the rules and resolving ambiguities, posing leading questions to students who are slow in catching on, and noting points that will need to be made when the class discusses the game. Because the teacher is not grading the student, the usual tension between them is considerably reduced.

WHAT THE PLAYERS LEARN

What do students learn by playing simulation games? What educational objectives can you reasonably expect a simulation game to accomplish? Many extravagant claims have been made in answer to these questions,[3] but in our opinion, there are some important types of educational objectives that simulation games actually achieve. Simulation games can increase the student's knowledge of terms and concepts, of specific facts, and of structures and relationships. They can help the student develop certain intellectual and social skills. And they can change the student's attitudes toward the things which are simulated in the game. In the next several pages, we will provide specific examples of these objectives and some simulation games which (we believe) actually achieve them.

Knowledge of Terms and Concepts

A simulation game can provide an especially effective means of expanding the student's vocabulary, as the game not only exposes the student to new terms and concepts but also requires him to use them correctly. For example, *Venture*, a business simulation, requires the players to use such terms as "depreciation," "working capital," "plowback," and "market research." A player must use these terms correctly in order to participate in the simulation.

Knowledge of Specific Facts

A simulation game can teach facts in the same way it teaches vocabulary: by presenting the information and requiring the players to use it. In *Life Career*, each team receives a 45-page school-job catalog containing information about 17 types of schools and approximately 100 occupations. For each type of school, the catalog gives admission requirements, costs, courses offered, and degrees granted. For each job, the catalog gives the educational requirements, typical starting salary, yearly raise, and top salary, total number of

---

[1] For further theoretical discussion of games as educational settings, see Coleman (1966) or Inbar and Stoll (1970).

[2] Soviet schools have a different use of competition and lean heavily on intergroup rather than interindividual contests for rewards, praise, and grades. For detailed comparison of American and Soviet classrooms, see Bronfenbrenner (1970).

[3] Chapter 5 presents a list of these claims and an evaluation of them in the light of the existing experimental evidence.

workers, and percentage of male and female workers. The players use this information in planning a career for their person.

Knowledge of Structures and Relationships

The structures and relationships of real life are represented in simulation games both in the rules and in the results of the players' decisions. By learning the rules of the game, the student learns the structure of the real situation as interpreted by the game designer. In fact, the game, by representing the structure of reality in a simplified form, makes the main points of the structure easier to learn. When the student plays the game and observes the results of his actions, he learns the cause-and-effect relationships that operate in the real situation.

For example, in *Life Career* the amount of satisfaction a person gets from his job depends on the educational level required by the job and the number of years the person has held the job. For lower-level jobs the scores decrease over time; for higher-level jobs the scores increase over time. (These scores are based on the results of sociological survey research.) The players who choose a lower-level job for their fictional person will then observe the decrease in his job satisfaction from year to year.

Intellectual and Social Skills

A simulation game teaches skills by providing the incentive to develop them and the opportunity to practice them. The incentive results from the fact that certain skills enable players to do well in the game. The opportunity to practice comes during the actual playing of the game. Simulation games can teach planning and resource allocation, persuasive skills (such as negotiation and bargaining), and a skill which we call "strategic anticipation," the ability to anticipate what another person will do in a given situation.[4] *Diplomacy* teaches all three of these skills. Planning and resource allocation are essential in positioning armies and fleets. Persuasive skills are necessary to secure alliances or nonaggression pacts and to hold other players to their agreements. Strategic anticipation is vital for survival in both diplomatic and military maneuvers.

Attitude Change

A simulation game can change a student's attitudes toward a real-life situation, not merely by providing new information, but by giving him a new way of looking at the situation. For example, in *Ghetto* the player takes the role of a resident of an inner-city slum. He may find himself unemployed and, in an effort to obtain the necessities of life, turn to "hustling" (a general term for illegal occupations). This strategy, in the game as in real life, combines the promise of high rewards with the risk of severe penalties. Although the player may

have heard or read of others who turned to crime for similar reasons, he will now have the experience of making that decision himself. We believe that this kind of experience can change a student's attitudes.

SIMULATION GAMES AND THE INQUIRY APPROACH

The *inquiry* approach to social studies places its emphasis on teaching the student to ask the right questions, rather than on requiring him to learn information. The student is expected to learn to read historical material the way a historian does, to analyze an economic situation the way an economist does, and so on.[5]

Do simulation games have a place in this approach? We think they do. Simulation games can be used to teach students to ask the same kinds of questions that social scientists ask about real social systems. One way to study the relationships in any kind of system is to try to predict the effects of changes in the system. For example, an economist might try to predict the effect of a tax reduction on employment. A sociologist might try to predict the effects of a strictly enforced fair-housing law on the residential patterns of different groups in a city. The teacher of a social studies class can lead the students to make the same kind of predictions about a simulation game they have played. To test the predictions, the class can make the specified change in the game, play the game again, and see what happens.

What kinds of changes would these be? One kind would be a change in resources available to the players at the start of the game. For example, in *SIMSOC*, the change might be in the number of "simbucks" the players begin the game with. In *Diplomacy*, the change might be in the number of supply centers in each country.

Another kind of change would be a change in the players' goals. This type of change could be made easily in *SIMSOC*, by assigning goals to the players instead of letting them choose their own. In *Life Career*, players might play the game once to try to get the greatest satisfaction for the eight years of the game; the next time they might try for the greatest expected satisfaction for the thirty years following the last year of the game.

A third kind of change would be a change in the rules. In *Diplomacy* a rule could be made to forbid secret talks between players. Or the rule might forbid *all* talks between players. In *SIMSOC*, the rules governing travel or the rule concerning the power of a group of players to set up a police force could be changed.

A fourth kind of change would be a change in the roles represented by different players in the game. For example, in *SIMSOC*, one of the

---

[4] See Schelling (1963).

[5] See Fenton (1967).

groups—perhaps the mass media—could simply be removed from the system. Or two or more of the original groups could be combined into a single group. In *Diplomacy*, a country could be removed from the game, just as Russia was taken out of World War I by the Bolshevik revolution in 1917. Or the armed forces of two countries could be combined under the command of one player.

When your class uses a simulation game in this way they will be using a technique that has recently become increasingly popular with social scientists—research with simulations. This technique is rather new in the social sciences, although physical scientists have long used models of the objects or processes they wish to study when experiments on the real objects or processes are either too costly or impossible. An example is the use of model airplanes in wind tunnels to study the behavior of real airplanes in flight. In the same sense, a social simulation is a model of a real social system. Some of the simulations that social scientists use for research are complex computer programs, but some are simulation games like those you may use in your classroom—and in some cases

they are the very same games. For example, James S. Coleman developed a mathematical theory of the behavior of legislators from his observations of players in the *Democracy* game.[6] Another classroom game which has been used for research on the behavior of political decision-makers is the *Inter-Nation Simulation*.[7]

Another way to fit simulation games into the inquiry approach is to use them as you would any other source of information. The rules of a game involve certain assumptions about the real situation that the game simulates. Often these assumptions are not explicitly stated. Just as you would lead your students to discover and question the unstated assumptions of a document or article or textbook chapter they have read, you can lead them to discover and question the unstated assumptions of a simulation game they have played. Remember that a simulation is based on only one of many possible interpretations of the situation it simulates. You can make this fact clearer to your students by following the simulation game with a reading assignment or film that presents a different interpretation.

STUDENTS' COMMENTS—PRO AND CON

(This selection of unedited comments, by junior high school, high school, and college students writing about several different games, illustrates the various ways students may react to a simulation game in the classroom.)

"Yes. I enjoyed the game. The game was more real than a textbook covering the same material, and it provided a fairly accurate 'real life situation' for the most part."

"I don't like the game any at all. It take to much time and to much thinking and its not any fun."

"I enjoyed it most because it was something you are doing, not just reading and hearing about it."

(Do you feel the game was a worthwhile activity?) "Yes. Because it wasn't as boring as the other stuff we do."

"We could have limited ourselves to textbooks, but I don't think we'd have gotten as much out of the course. By playing games we were able to observe the social behavior of the others in class, and with the post-game discussion we were able to analyze it. I believe it is more useful to observe and participate in social behavior than just read about it."

"I did not like them because I didn't have a understanding what the games were for."

"With the games a person can get a better understanding of the lesson than by the teacher teaching it. With the games you understand what was going on. And once you learned the rules of the game you could learn the facts better and faster. You didn't have a teacher standing over you talking a lot of stuff you really wasn't interested in and they weren't making interesting. With the games you learned the work as well as having fun in doing it."

"My opinion of this game is that outside of being cruddy, it smells. If this game were to replace the traditional way of teaching, I would drop out."

"In games in which bartering was the primary object, I became aware of the feelings of helplessness at not being able to obtain what was necessary for achieving my goal. Also in several instances of trying to create a situation whereby every one would have equal distribution of power, I became more aware of the naivete of this idealistic notion."

"I didn't enjoy playing any of the games, because I didn't learn anything."

"I think you learn a lot but I don't like the way you play. The hours are too long. You have to rush to much and if you don't do good the counselor get mad."

"In the game on economics, I don't feel I learned anything except how to swindle people. But I found it very enjoyable."

---

[6] See Coleman (1969).

[7] See Coplin (1970), Druckman (1968), and Guetzkow (1963).

REFERENCES

Bronfenbrenner, Urie. 1970. *Two Worlds of Childhood.* New York: Russell Sage.

Coleman, James S. 1966. "Introduction: In Defense of Games." *American Behavioral Scientist* 10:3-4.

_____. 1969. "Games as Vehicles for Social Theory." *American Behavioral Scientist* 12:2-6.

Coplin, William D. 1970. "Approaches to the Social Sciences Through Man-Computer Simulations." *Simulation and Games* 1:381-410.

Druckman, Daniel. 1968. "Ethnocentrism in the Inter-Nation Simulation." *Journal of Conflict Resolution* 12:45-68.

Fenton, Edwin. 1967. *The New Social Studies.* New York: Holt.

Guetzkow, Harold, et al. 1963. *Simulation in International Relations: Development for Research and Teaching.* Englewood Cliffs, N.J.: Prentice-Hall.

Inbar, Michael, and Stoll, Clarice S. 1970. "Games and Learning," *Interchange* 1:53-61.

Schelling, Thomas. 1963. *The Strategy of Conflict.* Cambridge, Mass: Harvard.

3 Using Simulation Games in the Classroom

SELECTING A GAME

In an ideal world a teacher would be able to reach for a volume entitled "Consumers' Reports of Simulation Games" and choose a "best buy" for his intended purpose. To date, no one has compiled all the information necessary for making well-balanced appraisals of all available simulation games.[1] We could list our favorite games (or the few we think are "losers"), but our list would probably be unfair because of the limitations of our experience; to evaluate a game fairly, one should first use it a number of times in an actual classroom situation, preferably with several kinds of students. Instead of attempting to evaluate specific games, we will try to describe criteria that you can use in selecting a game. These criteria can be grouped into three general categories: the suitability of the game for your particular purpose, its value as a teaching device, and its cost.

The most obvious criterion for selecting a simulation game (or any other teaching device) is that it must help you teach something you want to teach. As any simulation game will emphasize some aspects of the real situation it simulates, at the expense of others, you will want to choose a game that emphasizes aspects of the real situation that you consider important and worth teaching.

The game you select must be playable in your classroom situation. The game should not require more players than you can provide. If your class is not large enough, you may be able to combine classes with another teacher for the game session. More often, though, you will have too many students for the game. There are several ways to get around this problem. One way, if you have enough sets of game materials, is to divide the class into groups of the proper size and give each group a set of materials. Another is to double up by having a team of two or three students play each role in the game. A third way (if your school situation permits it) is to split the class, sending half the students to another room to work on independent projects while the other half plays the game. On another day, the two groups can exchange tasks.

The game must be playable in the time you have available. If your students change classes and the class periods are fairly short, this requirement can be an obstacle. Fortunately, many games can be played in installments; the students can begin where they stopped at the end of the previous day's class. In games that simulate sessions of Congress (or some other legislative body), the playing time can be shortened and the game made more realistic by having the players use out-of-class time for negotiation, bargaining, "log-rolling," and the like. The game would then occupy part of three class periods: Bills would be introduced and referred to committee the first day, reported out of committee the second day, and brought to the floor for a roll call vote the third day. In general, though, it is better not to interrupt a game. Double-length periods, if you have any, are excellent for simulation games.

Games that can be completed in a fairly short time have another advantage in that they can be played several times. By playing a game several times, the students can try out different combinations of strategies and learn their consequences. If the game has different roles, the students can exchange roles and thus experience the situation from several points of view.

The game should not require more space than your classroom provides, unless you have access to a larger room (perhaps a gymnasium, auditorium, or cafeteria). The game should not require any special furniture or equipment that you cannot easily obtain. For example, some games require a desk calculator; others require a large table or desks with level tops (although the floor may be adequate).

The game should not create more noise and disorder than you (or your administrators or fellow teachers) can tolerate. In the authors' opinion, noise in the classroom is not necessarily a bad thing, for it often indicates that the students are actively involved in the lesson. However, we also recognize that many teachers are under pressure from administrators or other teachers to keep the noise down. Games often create excitement, with several people talking at once. There are ways to minimize the noise that results (a few are suggested later in this chapter), but some games are inherently noisier than others. In general, games with a great

---

[1] A great deal of useful information can be found, however, in Zuckerman and Horn (1973).

deal of interaction among players, especially games that involve negotiation or bargaining by several players at once, tend to be the noisiest. The quietest games are those in which communication among the players is restricted by the rules of the game.

The game you select must also be suitable for your students. They must be capable of learning to play it without great difficulty. Most games designed for use in schools provide a fairly good guideline by indicating the range of ages or grade levels for which the game is intended. What really matters, though, is the ability of the students; a game intended for grades seven to nine will probably work quite well with fifth graders who can read and reason at an eighth-grade level.

The educational purpose of a simulation game is to teach students about the real situation that it simulates. Therefore the game must provide (as much as possible) a true and useful picture of the real situation. The outcome of the game should be determined by the same factors (or at least some of the same factors) that determine the outcome of the real situation. The decisions which the players have to make in the game should be among those that the participants in the real situation must make, and these decisions should have the same results (both immediate and long-range) as they would in the real situation. These characteristics of a simulation game are difficult to evaluate without playing the game, but a careful reading of the rules may reveal some of the more serious distortions of reality.

The game must be structured so that the students can learn by playing it. It should provide both the opportunity and the incentive for learning. Success in the game should depend on learning the things that the game is supposed to teach. The game should require the players to make decisions, solve problems, plan strategies, acquire information, or exercise skills. If the game only requires the players to throw dice and move tokens, then all that the players will learn is throwing dice and moving tokens.

A simulation game is a learning activity, but it is also a game. Just as a textbook cannot be effective unless it is readable, a simulation game cannot be effective unless it is playable. A careful study of the rules and materials of a game can often reveal much about its playability. The rules should be clearly written and easy to understand. If they are long and detailed, a brief summary of the rules should be available to each player (or printed on the playing materials). If there is none, you can write one in your own words, reproduce it, and hand it out to the class on the first day you use the game.

More important than the way the rules are written is the information they give you about the way the game is played. As you read the rules, you should watch for indications of certain specific drawbacks. One very important flaw in many games is idle time for the players. It is most likely to occur when the sequence of events contains a step in which some of the players do not participate. Idle time may also occur when some action must be performed by each player in turn, one at a time. The problem is especially acute in games played by large groups; at any given time there are more players waiting, and each player must wait longer for his turn.

Some simulation games require the players to make long or complex calculations that slow up the game and often produce errors; their inclusion in a game must be considered a drawback unless one purpose of the game is to teach the players to do these calculations. If you want to use a game which involves a number of calculations, you may find it worthwhile to perform the calculations in advance and list the results in a table which the players can consult during the game.

Well-designed playing materials can make a game easier to play and to administer. In general, the fewer pieces there are, the easier the game will be to administer. If there are several different kinds of pieces, a box with compartments will help keep them in order. The game will be easier to play if the different pieces are distinguished by color, shape, size, or clearly discernible pictures. If the pieces are identifiable only by printed labels, the players may get them mixed up during the game.

A game intended for classroom use should include a teacher's manual. (It may be designated "director's manual" or "co-ordinator's manual.") It should contain instructions for administering the game and a clear statement of the educational objectives of the game. Ideally, it should also contain a list of suggested questions for class discussion, suggestions for related supplementary activities, an explanation of any difficult or unfamiliar concepts incorporated in the game, a glossary of technical terms related to the subject of the game, and a bibliography of recommended books, articles, and teaching aids.

One other criterion for selecting a game is cost. In estimating the cost of a game, remember to multiply the item cost by the number of sets you will need for your class. Also remember that the long-range cost of the game will depend on the durability of the materials, the likelihood of their being lost, and the cost of replacing forms and score sheets that are used up.

How much do simulation games actually cost? There are two figures which you should take into account. The first is the price of a single set—the smallest amount that will enable you to try the game with your students. The second is the cost per student per hour—the actual cost of using the game in your classes. The variation between games in the price of a single set is tremendous, but the variation in cost per student per hour is considerably less. A simple game which can be played in one forty-minute period, containing materials for six players, may sell for as little as $1.50. A complex game which can accommodate from thirty to fifty players and requires eight to twelve hours to play may cost as much as $150. Yet the cost per student per hour for the two games would be approximately the same!

Unfortunately, you may have to decide whether or not to buy a game without ever seeing it. Publishers cannot generally afford to send simulation games out on approval because of their relatively high cost and low volume of sales. For a very few games (usually the larger, more expensive ones), you can buy an inexpensive sample materials kit and decide on the basis of the sample materials whether or not to invest in the game. Otherwise you will have to rely for information on advertisements and promotional literature, reviews of the game in professional magazines and journals,[2] and the advice of colleagues who have seen the game, played it, or used it in class.

ADMINISTERING A GAME

Before attempting to administer a simulation game in your classes you should understand the game yourself. You need not be an expert on every detail, but you must have a general understanding of the way the game works and what the players must do. The best way to learn a game is to play it, but if you cannot find enough others who are interested enough to spare the time, you should do your best to figure out the game by studying the rules and materials.

You can often save time, especially when you are using a complicated game, by preparing materials in advance. For example, if each player starts the game with a certain number of each type of token, you can have the tokens counted out and placed in envelopes ahead of time. Play money also can be counted out in advance and placed in separate bundles, one for each player. Cards can be sorted and shuffled. Arithmetic calculations can be done in advance and listed in a table. Often students will be willing to help with tasks of this type.

On the day you introduce the game in class, you will probably want to begin by telling the students what the game is about. *Keep it brief.* Three or four sentences should do the job; simply tell the class what real-life situation the game simulates, who the players represent, and what their goals as players will be. (You may also want to warn them to keep the noise down.)

The next step is to have the players divide into groups and choose roles. You may assign the students to groups or let them form their own. You should decide in advance what size groups to use and whether or not to have the students double up on the roles. Doubling up helps the slower students gain confidence, although it can sometimes prove awkward because of physical crowding. If you decide to have the students double up or if the

game is played in teams, it is a good idea not to let the most able students work together the first time the class plays the game. Pairing a bright student with a slower one will make for more even competition and will help the slower students learn the game more easily.

Each group should have one student who is responsible for administering the game and teaching it to the other students. This student should be one who is familiar with the game or one who catches onto new things quickly and explains them well to others. He should be responsible for interpreting the rules in case of a dispute or misunderstanding; tell him to ask you for help if he has trouble making a decision.

The better your student administrators understand the game, the better they will be able to explain it to the other students. Therefore, it is a good idea to give them a chance to play the game (or at least to study the rules and materials) before you introduce the game to the whole class. You may be able to have the student administrators come in after school to play the game; if not, you may be able to release them from other class activities to study the game. Or you may want to give them the game to study or play at home.

In case you have to keep the noise level down to avoid disturbing neighboring classes, you can assign one student in each group to be responsible for keeping the group orderly and reasonably quiet. This student may or may not be the one who administers the game, but he must be one that the others will listen to. If the group gets too noisy, remind him to quiet the others down. Delegating this responsibility to a student in each group should help keep the noise down. Of course, if the noise from any group remains too loud, you can end the game for that group while allowing the other groups to play on. The combination of student authority and the threat of ending the game should prevent noise from becoming an obstacle to the use of a game in class.

While the students are playing the game, move around the room from one group to another, answering the students' questions about the rules. If a group seems to be having trouble, ask if there is something they don't understand. Sometimes the rules will be ambiguous or a situation may arise which was not anticipated by the rules. If this happens, go ahead and make up a rule; the rules of a game are not sacred. If you notice a group playing incorrectly, don't correct them unless they seem to be uncertain as to what they are doing. You can correct their misunderstanding of the rules during the class discussion afterwards. The students will learn more by playing the game incorrectly than by trying to master every detail of the rules before starting to play.

Don't coach. Try to help the players understand the rules, but let them plan their own strategies. They may try to get you to tell them the "right" move; resist the temptation. Students learn when they have to make decisions on the basis of the information they have available, trying to an-

[2] The journal *Simulation and Games* (Sage Publications, Inc., 275 South Beverly Drive, Beverly Hills, California 90212) has a regular "Simulation Review" column which contains evaluations of specific games.

ticipate the results of each possible strategy. They learn much less when they use a certain strategy because the teacher recommended it.

The following excerpt, taken from the instructor's manual for *SIMSOC*, provides a good example of the right way to respond to students' questions before and during a game. In this example, "I" stands for "instructor"; "S" stands for student. (Remember that *SIMSOC* is intended for senior high school and college students; teachers with younger students will have to phrase their answers in simpler language.)

S: I don't understand when a police force has the right to arrest somebody. Can they just arrest anybody they please for any reason?
I: That's right, if they follow the procedure outlined here.
S: Well, what's to keep someone from starting a police force for the purpose of getting the money of some rich person?
I: There is nothing in the rules against doing that but that doesn't mean it will necessarily happen. But it could happen.
S: You mean if someone wouldn't do what I wanted, I could just start a police force and force him to do it?
I: I can't answer that really because forcing him to do something is not part of the rules. The rules say that you could restrict his travel, keep him from holding any official position, and have all his resources confiscated including his salary, tickets, and so forth. They don't say that he has to do anything you want him to do.
S: Why would someone want to start a police force except for confiscating someone else's resources?
I: I can't answer that. Let's just say that there are many other possible reasons besides that one.
S: It seems to me that this police force rule will mean that the society will turn out to be a police state.
I: Maybe and maybe not. But there is no point in our speculating about it. We'll just have to wait and see what happens. The important thing now is for you to understand what the rules on the police force allow you to do, not to anticipate what will happen when you start playing.

Many games have rules that specify time limits for certain activities. These time limits may be intended to force the players to make decisions under pressure (if the participants in the real situation must do so), or they may be intended only to keep the game moving. In either case, they should be leniently enforced at first, when the students are learning to play the game. Once the students have learned to play the game, all time limits should be strictly enforced.

Simulation games are generally most effective as teaching devices when the players have a chance to play them several times. Usually the students will need one playing just to learn how to play a game. They will need at least one more playing to develop sound strategies. Only after the students feel they have mastered the game will they be willing to experiment with strategies that appear unsound, and they can learn a great deal from this kind of experimentation. If the game has several different roles, each student should have a chance to play each role (or as many different roles as time permits). Class discussion between playings of the game will allow the students to benefit from each other's experience and thus enable them to learn more from each additional playing of the game.

CLASS DISCUSSION OF THE GAME

Possibly the greatest advantage of simulation games as a technique for teaching social studies is the degree to which they stimulate discussion among students. A large part of the learning that results from simulation games probably occurs during the discussions that follow the playing of the game. The discussions give the students a chance to compare strategies and thus benefit from each other's experience. Often a game moves so quickly that the players have no chance to think about the relationships operating in the game. The post-game discussion gives them this chance; it allows the students who have "caught on" to the game to point out to the other students the relationships they have observed. Class discussion is also the primary means of integrating a game into the course of study, by making the students aware of the connections between the game and their other classroom work.

The following suggested plan for discussion is meant to be general enough to apply to almost any simulation game. Although some of the suggested questions may be irrelevant to some games, most of the questions should be relevant to most games. Therefore the questions are expressed in the most general form possible. It will be up to you to fill in the details, according to the game you are using.

The first phase of the discussion should concentrate on the game itself. Begin by asking the students about their experiences in the game: What strategies did you use? What were the results? If you could play the game again, what would you do differently?

Then ask the students to generalize from these experiences (and their own): What is the best strategy in the game? Is it better to take chances or to "play it safe?" Are different strategies better for different players? If so, what should your choice of strategy depend on?

Next, explore the relationships among rules, strategies, and results by suggesting a way in which the rules might be changed. Suppose this change were made: What would be the best strategy then?

How would the results of the game be different? Which players would the change help, and which ones would it hurt?

Finally, try to lead the students to state the cause-and-effect relationships that operate in the game. These relationships may be quite complex, involving the rules of the game, the player's decisions, chance events, and, of course, the final outcome. A student who can state these relationships in his own words and illustrate them with accounts of his own and others' experiences in the game has truly learned the game. (However, it is not necessarily true that a student who cannot state these relationships in words has failed to learn the game. The problem is often a lack of verbal facility. A student who consistently performs well in the game can also be said to have learned the game.)

The second phase of the discussion should consist mainly of comparisons of the game with the real-life situation it represents. Here the students can use their knowledge of the real situation, which they have gained from their other classroom activities and their experiences outside of school. Begin by asking questions to make sure the students have understood what features of the real situation are represented by each feature of the game: What real-life persons are represented by each player in the game? What things in the real-life situation do the tokens in the game represent? What does the game board show about the structure of the real situation? What does each area of the board represent? What does each step in the order of play represent? Often students who have mastered the game will be unaware of the significance of many of its features, particularly when concrete objects in the game represent abstract quantities in the real-life situation. For example, a student who plays a game in which colored chips represent "political influence" may not know what political influence in the real world is, and why it is effective.

Next, lead the students to question and attempt to justify the rules of the game. Choose a certain rule and ask: Why does the game include this rule? What is there in the real situation that has the same effect that this rule has in the game?

Ask the students for their opinion of the scoring system: Is it realistic? Is it fair? Is the real situation fair?

Proceed to a comparison of strategies in the game with those in the real-life situation: If you were in the real situation, would you have done what you did in the game? If not, why not? Do people in the real situation make their decisions the way the players in the game do? Should they? Do people in the real situation ever make unwise decisions? If so, why? What would happen if people with experience in the real situation were to play the game? What strategies would they use? Could they learn anything about themselves by playing the game?

If the players have understood the cause-and-effect relationships in the game, they should be able—with a little help—to recognize them in the real situation. They should also be aware of the limitations of the game, the elements of the real situation that have been overemphasized, underemphasized, or omitted. You may ask: What makes the most difference in deciding the outcome of the game? What makes the most difference in deciding the outcome of the real situation? Has anything that matters in the real situation been left out of the game? How important is luck in the game? How important is luck in the real situation? A final point that should not be ignored is the players' feelings while playing the game: What were some of the things that happened to you in the game, and how did they make you feel? Do you think people in the real situation feel the same way?

DESIGNING SUPPLEMENTARY ACTIVITIES

No game can teach everything worth knowing about the situation it simulates. Supplementary activities related to the content of the game can help fill the gaps in information presented in the game, provide those details that are lacking in the game, present an alternative point of view, and give the students a chance to experiment with the rules of the game and test its assumptions.

One obvious supplement is the use of audiovisual materials about the situation represented in the game. Films and filmstrips can provide a detailed picture of objects which are only symbolically represented in the game, and the game can make the students aware of the relationships among objects pictured in the film. A film can be shown either before or after the game. If you show it before the game, it may help the students learn the game, but it may also predispose them to behave in a certain way in the game, and thus reduce the variety of strategies they try.

Readings are another valuable supplement to a simulation game. While in one sense the game presents as many different points of view as it has different roles, in another sense, it presents only one point of view, that of the game designer. Readings can help to correct this imbalance, especially if they concentrate on aspects of the real situation that are ignored or oversimplified in the game. For example, in *Diplomacy*, when two armies of equal strength move against each other, the result is a standoff, which causes no change on the *Diplomacy* board and no loss to either player. The resulting situation is the same as if neither player had ordered his army into action. The players may be only vaguely aware that such a standoff would in real life mean thousands of deaths and tremendous destruction and suffering. To emphasize this point, you might have them read a selection from Remarque's *All Quiet on the Western Front*.

If your students have the necessary reading ability, they may appreciate excerpts from writings by participants in the real situation, because of their authenticity. A game on politics could be supplemented by assigned selections from the writings of real politicians; a game on labor-management relations could be supplemented with excerpts from speeches by union leaders and corporation executives.

Every simulation game is based on assumptions about the real situation. Usually these assumptions are not stated explicitly, but are implicit in the rules, scoring formulas, chance devices (such as spinners or cards), and so on. If you can identify these assumptions, you may be able to devise activities in which the students do research to test them. Information against which to test the game's assumptions may be found in books, newspapers, magazines, journals, and government documents. The students may also collect their own data by taking a poll, conducting interviews, or observing and recording some facet of people's behavior. For example, the *Democracy* game assumes that voters who are satisfied with the actions of Congress will vote to re-elect their Congressman and that voters who are dissatisfied will vote against him. This assumption can be tested by means of a poll of adults who voted in the last congressional election.

Some simulation games are ideal for experimentation, and often the students can learn more from changing a game than from playing it again in its original form. Try this exercise: Propose one or more simple changes in the rules of the game, and have each student make a written prediction as to the effect of these changes on the outcome of the game. Then have the students play the game, with the changes, to test the predictions. To avoid self-fulfilling prophecies, have two sets of proposed changes. Let one group make predictions for the first set of changes and play the game with the second set of changes, while another group does the opposite. Thus each group will test the other group's predictions.

Another way to use a game is to have the students change it to simulate a different situation. Creating a new version of the game can be a class project; it will require a little bit of ingenuity and a lot of research. For example, a game that simulates a session of Congress, using current issues, could be modified to simulate a session of Congress at some other time in history. A game designed to simulate a real or fictitious international crisis could be modified to simulate a different crisis in another part of the world. When the students have finished modifying the game, they can play the new version they have created. If the class is large, you can divide it into two or more groups and have each group create its own variation of the game, modifying it to fit a specific situation. Then each group can play the other group's variation.

EVALUATING STUDENT LEARNING

In general, it is *not* a good idea to give students grades based on their performance in the game, for two reasons. First, a student's performance in a game is often a poor indication of what he has learned from the game. Success in many games depends heavily on luck or on the actions of other players. Players with certain roles often have a considerable advantage over the others. A student can perform poorly in a game and yet learn more from the experience than another student who receives a higher score. Second, if students know they are being graded on their performance in a game, they tend to be overly cautious in their choice of strategies while playing the game. By failing to explore the riskier and less conventional strategies open to them, they fail to learn as much as they would if the game were "only a game."

After your students have played and discussed a simulation game, you will probably want to know what (if anything) they learned from the game, in order to evaluate the success of the game as a teaching device. Unfortunately, pencil-and-paper tests place simulation games at a disadvantage when compared with other forms of instruction. Objective tests require the student to supply several small items of information, one at a time. Textbooks, lectures, and films present information in this way; simulation games do not. Essay tests require the student to organize his knowledge into a verbal communication. Textbooks, lectures, and most films organize information into verbal communication; simulation games do not.

Nevertheless, it is possible to construct tests of either type, objective or essay, that will test some of the things that students learn from the game. Many simulation games provide a setting in which students can learn to use new terms and concepts. Though the students may not have memorized definitions of these concepts, they should be able to recognize or supply examples of them. A simulation game also provides an excellent way for students to learn the cause-and-effect relationships that operate in the real-life situation. These relationships can be converted into test items by stating them in the "if . . . then . . ." form, presenting the "if" clause and having the students supply the "then" clause. Simple relationships can be presented as single objective-test items; more complex relationships can be presented as essay items. Sometimes a complex relationship can be broken down into a series of simpler relationships, which can then be presented as objective-test items.

Another way to test the effectiveness of a simulation game is to construct a different simulation exercise that requires for success the skills and behaviors that the students are supposed to learn from the original game. This exercise need not be a game; it should be constructed so that the student's success depends as much as possible on his own actions, as little as possible on the actions of others, and not at all on chance. One example of such a test is that used by Anderson (1970) in a research study. Anderson was trying to measure the effectiveness of the game *Consumer* for teaching credit-shopping behavior. He constructed a simulation exercise in which the student was faced with the need to buy a car. The student received a profile sheet which contained detailed information on his transportation needs and financial resources. Three different types of car were available, and the student could finance his purchase with any of three lending agencies, each offering three different credit plans, a total of twenty-seven possible combinations. The student could receive information about the credit plans only by "visiting" the lending agencies. Each of the twenty-seven possible combinations of car, agency, and credit plan was rated in advance according to its suitability to the situation described in the profile sheet. The student's score was the rating of the combination he chose. Anderson also recorded the number of agencies the student "visited" before making his choice.

Some simulation games are intended to change the attitudes of those who play them. You can evaluate the success of a game in changing your students' attitudes by using questionnaires similar to those that social scientists use in survey research. Most of these require the person whose attitude is being measured to express agreement or disagreement with each of several statements on a particular subject. Administering an attitude questionnaire to the students before they play the game and again after the game will give you an idea of the extent to which the game has changed their attitudes.[3] In constructing your questionnaire, try to have about half the statements express positive attitudes and the other half indicate negative attitudes. Also try to avoid presenting the statements in any systematic order. If you suspect that your students may be reluctant to express their true attitudes on the subject, have them answer the questionnaire anonymously, and design it so that the students can answer it with a minimum of writing. There are several ways to make sure that the responses will remain anonymous. One way is to assign each student a code number at random by means of numbered cards. Shuffle the cards and hand them out face down, one to each student. Have the students record their numbers and use them on the questionnaires instead of their names.

As the effectiveness of a game may depend on the students' understanding of it, you may find it helpful to give, in addition to your other tests, a test on the game itself. Fletcher (1968) has suggested four categories of test items to measure four different levels of understanding a simulation game.

The first category consists of items which test the students' knowledge of the facts and rules of the game. These questions show whether the student knows what is permitted in the game and what is possible in the game. For example:

In the *Diplomacy* game, does a player have to keep an agreement he makes with another player?

(A) Yes
(B) No
(C) Only if the agreement is made for a limited time.
(D) Only if the agreement is made public by announcing it to the other players.
(Correct answer: B)

The second category consists of items designed to show whether the student understands the strategies of the game. These questions may require the player to state general principles of strategy or to apply these principles to specific situations in the game. Another example from *Diplomacy*:

Which country would probably be most interested in a nonaggression treaty with Italy?

(A) Turkey
(B) Russia
(C) England
(D) France
(Correct answer: D)

The third category consists of items designed to show whether the student understands the structure of the game. These items require the student to predict the effects of a change in some part of the game. For example (continuing with *Diplomacy*):

Suppose that Turkey had only two supply centers, instead of three. Which countries would be helped most by this change?

(A) Russia and Austria
(B) Germany and Italy
(C) England and France
(D) All six countries would be helped about the same amount.
(Correct answer: A)

The fourth category consists of items designed to see if the student understands the analogies between the game and the real situation it represents. These items may require the student to identify the real-life objects represented by the various game materials. They may require him to state the reasons for certain specific rules. Or they may require him to evaluate these rules on the basis of his knowledge of the real situation, as in the following examples:

For each of these rules of *Diplomacy*, tell in one short sentence whether the rule is realistic or unrealistic, and why:

Players do not have to announce the agreement they make. (Realistic, because secret alliances existed in 1900.)
All countries except Russia begin the game with the same number of supply centers. (Unrealistic, because Germany and England

---

[3] This is not a rigorous experimental design. For a discussion of its weaknesses, see Campbell and Stanley (1966), pp. 7-12.

were much more powerful than Austria, Italy, and Turkey.)

These four types of questions can be quite helpful in diagnosing students' failures to learn from the game. If, after playing the game, the students have not learned the facts of the real situation, the reason may be that they have not learned the facts and rules of the game. On the other hand, it may be that they do not understand the analogies between the game and the real situation. Similarly, if they have not learned the strategies used in the real situation, they may have failed to master the strategies of the game, or they may have failed to grasp the analogies which would enable them to see why the same strategies that work in the game also work in the real situation. And if they have not learned the structure of the real situation, they may have failed to learn the structure of the game, or they may not understand the analogies by which the structure of the game represents the structure of the real situation.

One final word of caution: simulation games are at least as varied as films or textbooks. If the first simulation game you use in class is a tremendous success, don't assume that all simulation games will work as well. Similarly, if the first simulation game you use falls flat, don't avoid all simulation games because of that one badly designed (or inappropriately selected) game. Remember also that the way you introduce and administer a game can have a tremendous effect on the way the students take to it. If you follow the suggestions presented in this chapter, you will be giving the game a fair chance to show what it can do for your class.

TEACHERS' COMMENTS— PRO AND CON

"They loved it. Even the students who did not do well wanted to play again."

"The second day 2 out of 114 students did not wish to play. Low levels were particularly motivated. Two of my lowest achievers *won* games. Most students were reluctant to quit."

"They were not overly excited; poor reaction from boys; lower ability students cannot grasp leader roles, therefore they do not learn that facet of game."

"The 'slower' students especially seemed to [be] motivated by this game."

"Reaction at the end of the first round was not good. However, at the end of the second round the students became very involved. Students responded differently, but almost all responded enthusiastically."

"It was confusing at first, but after the first day the students enjoyed it."

"All students enjoyed it, though slower students took longer to learn to play it and grumbled while learning."

"They loved it! . . . role playing was [the] most spontaneous I have ever observed."

"Most responded according to their personality. Said they played it the way they would actually do it in life."

"Excited, active groups. But in each group there were some who took the road of least resistance and did what others told him to do."

"Students took a very serious approach to the game. Even emotionally upset kids were sober about choices for another's life."

"One or two students did shine as they had not before this activity."

"Students for the most part reacted favorably. Took longer for slower students to grasp meaning of game."

"I found that students of lower ability could respond to the game very quickly and develop strategy."

"Slower section took longer to learn to read graphs, however caught on to strategy much faster."

"The game took much explanation and pre-study; however, it worked satisfactorily for crystallizing all the facts and generalizations learned."

"A lot of reading to prepare myself to administer the game. In fact I put it off until the end of the year. I felt that it was so much to read and to have to know. I finally made myself do it as $25 is a lot for a game you don't use. I was pleasantly surprised to find the girls could take the reins and go to it and that all my worrying and work was unnecessary."

"I had few problems in instituting the game because I spent a lot of time preparing my preparation for the class, so that each student understood his role before the game started. This may have been wrong. I think that confusion at the beginning of the game is sometimes beneficial because the student benefits from just figuring out the principles of the game. The problem is that students who are totally confused may lose interest right away. I found this time that the students lost some interest towards the end of the game . . . ."

REFERENCES

Anderson, C. Raymond. 1970. "An Experiment on Behavioral Learning in a Consumer Credit Game." *Simulation and Games* 1: 43-54.

Campbell, Donald T., and Stanley, Julian C. 1966. *Experimental and Quasi-experimental Designs for Research.* Chicago: Rand McNally.

Fletcher, Jerry L. 1968. *The Effects of Two Elementary School Social Studies Games: An Experimental Field Study.* Unpublished doctoral dissertation, Harvard University.

Zuckerman, David W., and Horn, Robert E. 1973. *The Guide to Simulations/Games for Education and Training.* Cambridge, Mass.: Information Resources.

4 Designing a Simulation Game

EDUCATIONAL OBJECTIVES

Like the creator of any other teaching aid, you, the game designer, must begin by identifying your educational objectives: What do you want the game to teach? The more clearly, precisely, and specifically you define your objectives, the more easily you can design a game to accomplish them. Your most difficult task in designing a simulation game will be to decide which aspects of the real-life situation to leave out, and this decision will depend on your objectives. In the course of designing the game, you may find that you cannot attain all of your original objectives without making the game so complex as to be unusable in the classroom. In that case, you will have to narrow your objectives or perhaps even change them altogether. Do not be discouraged! A simulation game that proves unsuitable for its original purpose often proves to be highly suitable for a different but related purpose.

If your main purpose in designing the game is to teach facts, concepts, or skills (rather than values or attitudes), then the best way to make sure the students learn what you want them to learn from the game is to structure the game so that success in the game depends on learning these facts, concepts, or skills. If, on the other hand, your main purpose is to change the students' attitudes, you should structure the game so that it will lead the students to act in ways that are inconsistent with the attitudes you hope to change. For either objective (especially the latter), the game must be believable; the students must believe that the game truly represents the real-life situation.

STRUCTURE OF THE GAME

After identifying your objectives as precisely as you can, you are ready to select the real-life situation you intend your game to simulate. In some cases this decision will follow from your objectives; in others, the objectives will suggest several possible situations for simulation. Where you have a choice of situations to simulate, you can make the job of game designing easier by choosing a situation you already know well, preferably one with obvious game-like characteristics. A game can be based on almost any real-life situation in which there is competition or conflict, such as an election, an international crisis, or the day-to-day operations of companies in a competitive industry. Successful games have also been based on situations that (in real life) do not necessarily involve competition or conflict, such as career planning, credit use, and economic development.

Roles

Once you have identified your objectives and chosen a situation to simulate, you are ready to begin the actual process of game designing. The first step is to identify the roles that the players will take in the game. In some simulation games all players take the same role; in others, they take different roles. But in any good simulation game, the players represent *only those persons or groups who can make decisions that affect the outcome* of the situation. Whether to cast the players in similar or different roles will be determined partly by the nature of the situation your game will simulate and partly by your own preferences. Remember, though, that students who play different roles in a game often learn different things from the game.

While it is important to avoid using players to represent persons who have no real control over the outcome, it is not necessary to use players to represent all persons or groups who can influence the outcome. Decisions of persons not represented by players can be programmed into the game by means which vary in complexity from a simple flip of a coin to long, intricate computer programs. (Some of these devices will be discussed later in this chapter, under "Formulas, Tables, and Graphs" and "Cards, Spinners, and Dice.")

Goals

After you have determined the roles that the players will take, determine each player's goals. These goals may be the same for players in different roles, or they may be different. In some simulation games, the players are given some freedom to select their own goals within a structure determined by the game designer. (This process is somewhat like bidding in bridge or calling one's shot in pool.)

The player's goals may be expressed in terms of a specific outcome: something that may or may not occur in the game and that the players seek to promote or prevent. Games in which the players' goals are of this type may have more than one winner. They may be structured so that the number of winners is not determined in advance; sometimes no players, sometimes one, sometimes more than one, and sometimes all of the players will win. Of course, the game designer may (if he chooses) identify the winner as the first player to make a certain event happen or the last one to permit it to happen (for example, the first to get a million dollars or the last to go bankrupt).

More often, each player's goal is to get a high (or low) score, expressed in some unit of measurement. These units may be either concrete or abstract; that is, they may represent tangible or intangible things in the real situation. Some examples of concrete units are dollars, votes, tons of goods produced (or consumed or possessed), and cities under one's control. Abstract quantities are usually expressed as "points" or "credits" and represent such things as power, prestige, and satisfaction. Remember that two players cannot compare their scores at the end of the game unless their scores are expressed in the same units.

Resources

Next, identify the resources available to each player: those things that he can use to influence the outcome in his favor. Resources are usually available in limited amounts and may be either tangible or intangible. Tangible resources could be money, land, people (workers, soldiers, or voters), factories, railroad lines, years of formal education, or personal possessions. Intangible resources could be influence or prestige. Time can also be a resource, especially when players have different amounts of it or can use it in different ways. Time as a resource may be represented by actual playing time or may be allocated in units representing hours, days, weeks, and so on. For example, in *Ghetto* each player receives a number of colored chips as his main resource. Each chip represents one hour per day of time available for school, work, or other activities. The players then invest their time in various activities by placing their chips on the corresponding sections of the playing board.

When you have identified the different kinds of resources, determine their relative importance in influencing the outcome. You may want to adjust the amounts of resources given to the players to give every player an equal chance to win, instead of trying to match the exact distribution of resources in the real situation. Or you may choose to exaggerate inequalities in the distribution of resources in order to increase the impact of the game on the players. However, either of these deliberate distortions of reality will make the game less valid (true-to-life) and may make it less believable. In

general, it is better to adjust the scoring system than to distort the distribution of resources. Sometimes it is not possible to adjust the scoring system (there may not be one); then you may have to choose between a game that is true to life and a game in which the players have an equal chance to win. If the main purpose of your game is education, rather than entertainment, you should do all you can to make the game true to life.

Determining the correct distribution of intangible resources presents a problem. You may know that one player should have more of a certain resource than another player but not know just how much more he should have. This problem must be solved by testing the game and observing the results.

Interactions

Determine the interactions among the persons (or groups) in the real-life situation. These are the ways in which each person's decisions and actions affect the others' chances for success.[1] Some of the interactions may depend on the actions of individuals; for example, if one person buys large amounts of a scarce commodity, there will be less of it for others to buy. Other interactions may involve the combined actions of many persons or groups; for example, if all the producers in an industry together produce too much of a certain type of merchandise, its price will fall. Interactions can be either *deterministic* or *probabilistic*. When they are deterministic, they happen the same way every time. When they are probabilistic, chance plays a part. In the production example, if the interaction were deterministic, the amount of merchandise produced would determine its price exactly. If the interaction were probabilistic, the price would vary because of other, unidentified factors, but the amount produced would determine the probability that the price would reach any given level.

Once you have identified the interactions in the real-life situation, try to reproduce them in the form of rules and formulas. Interactions involving individuals may be expressed in rules such as: "If player A does x, then Player B cannot do y," or "If Player A does x, then any other player who does y must pay him n dollars." These rules may promote co-operation among the players by providing ways for them to exchange or combine resources. They may also promote competition by preventing players from combining resources.

In general, *the rules of the game should not forbid any actions except those that would be impossible in the real situation.* Actions that are discouraged in the real situation by fear of harm or punishment should be discouraged by corresponding penalties in the game.

[1] Some games have no interaction among players. Abt (1968, p. 68) has referred to such games as "showdown" games.

In this stage of designing the game—identifying the interactions and transforming them into rules—your knowledge of the real situation will be crucial. It is not enough to observe that a certain person in the real situation typically behaves in a certain way. You must have a theory about why that person behaves in that way and what would happen if he did not behave in that way. Only then can you construct rules that will lead the players to behave in the same way as the real persons they represent, for the same reasons.

This problem is particularly acute in historical games, which often simulate a particular situation that existed only once and was resolved a certain way. You will find yourself making many assumptions and educated guesses to reproduce the interactions that would have resulted from decisions that were never made. If your guesses are wrong, your game will bear little relation to historical reality. Yet, if you do not make the attempt, your game will not be a game at all, but a script by which players act out a predetermined course of events.

Sequence of Events

Determine a sequence of events for the game. This sequence can be either a repeating cycle or a single chain of events, depending on the real-life situation. You may find that events that take place at the same time in the real situation cannot conveniently be made to happen at the same time in a game. (For example, two nations at war may move their armies into battle at the same time.) Or you may find that the situation you intend to simulate consists of several continuous processes (for example, production, distribution, and consumption of goods). In these cases you cannot simply copy the sequence of events from the real situation. But you may be able to establish a logical order; for example, even though production, distribution, and consumption all go on at once, any particular item must be first produced, then distributed, then consumed. Or you may have to establish an arbitrary order; for example, country A may move a certain number of units, then country B may move the same number of units.

Ending the Game

Determining the end of the game may pose special problems. If the process you intend to simulate has a natural conclusion (for example, an election campaign concludes with the election), there will be no problem. Most real-life situations do not conclude so neatly. If your game simulates a situation that does not have a natural conclusion, you will have to define the point at which the game is over. This point could come at the end of a specified amount of time (as in football or basketball), or at the end of a certain number of repetitions of a repeating cycle of events (as in baseball), or when one player has reached a certain score (as in volleyball or table tennis). The problem is that

any artificial means for ending the game may cause the players to use special end-game strategies that would not make sense in the real-life situation.

There are three main ways to deal with this problem, and none of them is entirely satisfactory. First, you can simply not tell the players when the game will end. Of course, there must be somebody—usually the person who administers the game—who either knows or decides when the game will end. The fault with this solution is that trying to guess when the game will end becomes part of the players' strategy. This condition is undesirable because it is unrealistic; in most real-life situations, the participants do not have to guess when the situation will end.

Second, you can use a random process to determine the end of the game. For example, the players may throw a die at the end of every round (perhaps after a certain number of rounds have already been played), and if a "one" or a "six" comes up, the game is over. This technique keeps the players from being able to guess when the game will end, but it creates administrative problems; nobody knows how long the game will take.

Third, you can adjust the scoring system to allow for events that would occur after the time period covered by the game. For example, debts and investments (in a game on economics) or political obligations (in a game on politics) would have a delayed payoff, and the scoring system must allow for such effects. The fault with this solution is that it often requires the game designer to set an arbitrary value on things whose value should be determined by the events of the game and the players' decisions. In short, there is no simple solution to the problem of end-game effects. Fortunately, these effects are seldom so great as to destroy the educational value of the game.

External Factors

The last step in determining the basic structure of the game is to identify the external factors in the real situation and incorporate them into the game. External factors are anything outside the players' decisions and actions that will affect the outcome. These factors include the decisions and actions of persons or groups not represented by players in the game. They also include the conditions existing in the environment that are beyond the players' control. For example, in an economics game in which the players represent small producers, the market prices of goods would be an external factor. In a game in which the players represent captains of clipper ships, wind and weather would be external factors.

The external factors in a simulation game can be either variable or constant. When the factors in the real-life situation vary, you will usually want to reproduce them as accurately as possible. However, in some cases you may want to hold constant in the game a factor that varies in real life, in order to make the game simpler and easier to play. In such games the players must be made aware (either before or after the game) of the distortion of reality.

Variable external factors will often interact with the players' decisions and actions. For example, the outcome of a battle will depend not only on the strategy and resources of the two opposing armies, but also on weather conditions. The outcome of an election will depend on the strategies and resources of the candidates, but also on news events that happen during the campaign. Like the interactions that involve only the players, the interactions between players' decisions and external factors may be either deterministic or probabilistic. In the military situation, the combination of strategies, resources, and weather conditions may determine the outcome of the battle (a deterministic interaction), or it may determine the probability of each of several possible outcomes (a probabilistic interaction).

Constant external factors will often limit or affect the players' actions. These are usually conveniently represented on a playing board (though they may occasionally require the actual physical separation or regrouping of the players, having them move their chairs or go to different rooms). If the most important of these factors are geographic, the playing board will probably take the form of a map. If the game simulates a fairly complicated sequential process, the board may take the form of a path diagram or flowchart. If the game simulates a situation in which the participants' actions are limited by the structure of an organization, the board may take the form of an organization chart. Other kinds of constant external factors will require other board layouts. If there are no important external factors that are constant, there may be no board at all.

MATERIALS

When you have the structure of the game fairly well established (in your mind or on paper) you can begin to worry about the actual game materials. Producing these materials (especially in quantity) can be extremely tedious and time-consuming. However, you may find that your students will enjoy the chore and will produce better materials than you could have made for yourself. Do not spend a great deal of time and effort in an attempt to produce attractive and durable materials for the first version of your game. You will probably find yourself redesigning the materials several times before you are satisfied with them.

Many simulation games require a way to represent the location of persons and objects. Usually this means a playing board. What material makes a good playing board? For the early trial versions of a game you will need a material that is cheap and easy to cut, color, and write on. For the later versions, which will probably be used several times, you will need a material that is attractive, durable, and easy to carry, store, and set up for playing.

Cardboard is ideal for preliminary versions of a game because it is cheap and easy to work with. Its main disadvantage is its lack of durability. Wood, metal, and pegboard are all more durable but much harder to work with. Soft materials like felt and thin vinyl are the most convenient to store and to transport but not as easy to work with as cardboard; they are easy to cut but hard to draw on.

Any person, object, or physical feature that stays in one place throughout the game should be drawn directly on the board. Persons or objects that move can be represented by markers or tokens. Checkers, pawns, and poker chips all make good tokens. You can also design and cut out your own cardboard tokens. Do not use tokens made of ordinary paper; they will blow all over the room. You can bond the paper to cardboard with rubber cement.

Attempts to keep the tokens from sliding on the board are probably more trouble than they are worth. You can use pegs for tokens, but you must then either use pegboard or drill or punch holes in the board wherever a token might be placed. Pins are a poor solution; they are easily lost and may tempt students to mischief.

A throwaway paper board on which players mark their paths with colored crayons or pencils eliminates the need for tokens; it has the additional advantage of providing a record of the players' moves. However, this technique has limitations. The boards must be easily reproduced. (If the board is large it can be reproduced in sections and pasted together.) The game must be such that the players' paths do not often cross or retrace; otherwise the players will have trouble finding their positions. And the record of the players' moves which the board provides can be unrealistic if the game simulates a situation in which the participants do not have this information.

If your game uses tokens, a box with a separate compartment for each type of token will help the players keep track of the tokens; the game will move faster and with less confusion, and fewer tokens will be lost.

Tokens or Score Sheets?

There are two main ways for players to keep track of the resources they have available and the rewards they accumulate; these are tokens and score sheets. Each has its advantages. Tokens are tangible. The players can see, touch, and handle them. A pile of tokens has a greater psychological effect (for most players) than a number on a score sheet. The physical act of counting and exchanging tokens also helps to keep errors from going unnoticed. On the other hand, each token is another piece of equipment for the teacher to worry about. Tokens can be lost or misplaced. They provide an easy way to cheat; a dishonest player can simply steal tokens from his neighbor. The use of tokens also requires that all quantities be expressed in small whole numbers; pencil-and-paper calculations permit greater precision.

Formulas, Tables, and Graphs

Your simulation game will probably involve mathematical relationships. These may be the same relationships that exist in the real-life situation, or they may arise from your attempt to put numerical values on intangible things such as political power or prestige. These mathematical relationships can be expressed in formulas, graphs, or tables. Your decision as to which of these to use will depend on the educational objectives of the game, the mathematical ability of your students, the complexity of the relationship you want to represent, and the degree of precision you require. Some games require that complex relationships be expressed with great precision; these games usually make use of computers. This technique, of course, is seldom a practical alternative for the classroom teacher.

Simple relationships that do not involve difficult or time-consuming arithmetic computation can be conveniently expressed as formulas. These formulas should be expressed in words, rather than mathematical symbols (unless one of your objectives is to teach the students to apply formulas expressed algebraically). For example, a scoring formula might be $S = 2P - Q$, where S = player's score, P = prestige points earned, and Q = influence points used. To express this formula in words, you could say: "To find your score, multiply the number of prestige points you earned by two; then subtract the number of influence points you used."

If the relationships in your game do require some arithmetic, you can make the game go more smoothly by doing all the calculations in advance and presenting the results in the form of tables. Tables also have the advantage of allowing you to include in the game some relationships that may be beyond the players' mathematical knowledge (for example, logarithmic functions or the normal probability curve). Tables also permit you to represent relationships observed directly from the real situation, even when these relationships cannot be conveniently expressed in a formula. A table is especially convenient when a single output variable is determined by two input variables. For example, "speed of travel" might be determined by "type of terrain" and "weather conditions." If the table becomes too large to read easily, you can use a sliding cover with a window that reveals only one column of the table at a time. (Such a cover can often be made easily from a nine-by-twelve-inch file folder.)

Graphs are another way of expressing mathematical relationships. While they are less precise than formulas or tables, they give the players a much clearer picture of the relationship. Like tables, they permit the use of relationships beyond the players' mathematical knowledge. The graphs used in a simulation game will almost always be line graphs. A graph is most convenient when a single output variable is determined by a single input variable.

Cards, Spinners, and Dice

Any source of uncertainty that exists in the real situation can be simulated by means of chance devices. Variable external factors such as weather, market conditions, or decisions of persons not represented by players can be determined in the game by chance devices. Chance devices are also used to determine the outcome of probabilistic interactions, that is, any combination of players' decisions and external factors that produces more than one possible outcome. If you know how often each condition or each outcome is likely to occur in real life, you can make the chance device reflect these probabilities. If not, you will have to make an educated guess. You can adjust the probabilities later, when you revise the game.

The three most common chance devices used in simulation games are chance cards, spinners, and dice; each has its advantages and disadvantages. The use of chance cards allows the player drawing a card to read the result directly from the card, without consulting a table or chart. The card can also carry a message to explain the result; these messages can add a feeling of realism or a touch of humor to the game. For example, instead of saying "The market price of your product drops ten cents," a card can say "Foreign competition drives the market price of your product down ten cents," or "The unpredictable buying habits of the fickle public have caused a drop of ten cents in the market price of your product."

If you use chance cards, the probability of each result will depend on the number of cards in the deck that produce that result. If a certain result should happen about one-fourth of the time, then one-fourth of the cards in the deck should produce that result.

Chance cards have disadvantages as well as advantages. Cards can get lost, and if they do, the probabilities of the results will change. Cards tend to wear out, to become bent, dog-eared, or otherwise marked. And, although cards are not difficult to produce by hand, the job is a tedious one. But the greatest disadvantage of chance cards is that they can be misleading. The player who draws an unlikely chance card may not realize his unusual luck, as he has no way of knowing how many similar cards are in the deck.

Spinners have the advantage of being highly visual. The base of a spinner is actually a circle graph that shows how likely it is that each result will happen. The players can see these probabilities by just looking at the spinner; as a result, they will be more likely to learn the probabilities by spinning the spinner than by drawing cards. This feature is especially important when the probabilities in the game are based on actual results from the real situation. Like chance cards, spinners may allow the result to be read directly, without consulting a table or chart. However, a spinner does not allow much room for explanations, and you may want to provide them in a separate key (which can be printed on the spinner base, next to the spinner circle).

The main disadvantages of spinners are their lack of precision and their tendency to be biased. Very small probabilities are difficult to indicate accurately on a spinner. Arguments between players may result when the pointer comes to rest near a boundary. Skillful players may be able to spin the pointer to make it more likely to stop where they want it to. The spinner itself may be unbalanced. For these reasons, spinners are less accurate than either cards or dice.

If you decide to use a spinner, the best way to make one is to take the metal pointer of a spinner from an old game and fasten it to a cardboard base with a paper fastener. Divide the spinner circle into sectors as you would any circle graph; for example, if a certain result should happen about one fourth of the time, its sector should be one-fourth of the circle, or ninety degrees.

Dice provide a closer approximation to pure chance than either chance cards or spinners. However, the dice can only produce a number, and this number is generally not meaningful in itself. In order to find out what event has resulted from the throw, the player must consult a table or chart on which the possible results are keyed to numbers on the dice. For example, in a game about state legislatures in which the governor's action is an external factor, the chart might look like this:

Number on Dice	Governor's Action
2, 3, 4, 5, 6, 7, 8	Governor signs bill
9, 10	Governor takes no action
11, 12	Governor vetoes bill

Another possibility is to use the number on the dice in a formula that transforms it into a meaningful number. For example, in a farming game in which the price of wheat varies from $1.50 to $2.00 per bushel, the rules might say, "Roll the (two) dice. Multiply the number on the dice by 5; then add 140 to find the price of wheat in cents per bushel."

Dice are usually read by adding the numbers on the dice. This method provides a distribution of numbers fairly close to a *normal* distribution; numbers in the middle of the range occur much more frequently than either very high or very low numbers. Because many quantities in real life are distributed in a similar manner (height of persons is one example), this method of reading the dice is useful for producing numbers to plug into formulas, as in the wheat-farming example. The more dice you use, the more closely the distribution of numbers will approximate a normal distribution.

When dice are read in the conventional manner (by adding the numbers), they do not provide as much flexibility as either chance cards or spinners in determining the likelihood of each result. However, there is another way of reading dice, which yields a large number of equally probable results (as does a deck of chance cards). This way requires the player to throw the dice one at a time and read the numbers in order; for example, a 3 on the first die and a 1 on the second would not be the same indicator as a 1 on the first die and a 3 on the second. When read in order, two dice yield thirty-six equally likely combinations (instead of the eleven unequally likely numbers that result when the two dice are added); the effect is the same as drawing a chance card from a deck of thirty-six cards. To have thirty combinations instead of thirty-six, you can have the rules say, "If you roll a six on the second die, roll it again." To have twenty-five combinations, you can have the rules say, "If you roll a 6 on either die, roll that die again."

There are still other ways to have the players read the dice. You can have them multiply the numbers on the dice, or select the higher (or lower) of two dice, or subtract the lower from the higher. Each method yields a different distribution. (And, of course, you can use more than two dice.)

Dice have some practical disadvantages. A player rolling the dice may accidentally knock tokens off the board. The dice may roll under the desk or table. And the mere presence of dice may be too great a distraction for students who associate dice with gambling; the students may begin shooting craps and forget about the simulation game.

WRITING THE RULES

There are many possible ways to organize the rules for your game; here is one way that has proved fairly easy for players to understand. (You may notice that in some ways it parallels the process of designing the game.)

First, briefly describe the real-life situation the game is intended to simulate.

Second, briefly state the object of the game: What is each player's goal?

Third, identify each of the materials: What does the board depict? What does each kind of token represent? What are the tables, graphs, score sheets, chance cards, and spinners used for? Do not give any detailed explanations yet; be as brief as possible.

Fourth, tell how to set up the game in order to start playing: What pieces go where? Who starts with what resources?

Fifth, state the order of play, that is, the sequence of events. State it as concisely and systematically as you can; simply list the steps in order, without explanation.

Sixth, taking each step in the order of play separately, explain in detail what the players are to do during that step. Here is where you tell how to use each of the materials; here is where you state the rules governing the interactions between players.

Seventh, tell how to end the game and compute the final scores.

Eighth, provide an example in which you describe a typical round played by a typical player; tell what he does in each step of the order of play.

One way to help players learn the rules of the game is to give each player a general, brief summary of the rules. Players can then consult the complete rules for details as the occasion arises. Another way is to print the most important rules directly on the playing materials. Sometimes they can be put on the board, sometimes in a "profile" (a sheet of paper or a folder which also gives the player the information that applies specifically to his role). Be selective in choosing which rules to print on these materials. Usually the most important ones will be the order of play (sequence of events) and the scoring formulas.

REVISING THE GAME

When you have determined the structure of your game, written the rules, and designed and made the materials, you are ready to begin the process of testing and revision. Designing a simulation game is not the sort of activity in which you can expect to get everything right the first time. Certain problems that were not apparent when you first designed the game will appear when the game is played. Your attempts to solve these problems may create other problems, perhaps more serious than the ones you first noticed. The first playing of a game is often the most discouraging moment of the game-designing process. Try to remember to "keep your eye upon the donut and not upon the hole." In other words, notice the features of the game that work, as well as those that do not. Use these successful features as a basis for designing your first revised version.

The testing and revision process usually requires several trial playings of the game with a good deal of work in between. However, the players can learn from an unfinished version of a game. In fact, if you ask your students for suggestions for revising the game, they may learn more from making and discussing these suggestions than they would from playing a finished version of the game.

The two main considerations in revising a simulation game are realism and playability.

REALISM

The word *realism*, when applied to simulation games, usually refers to a combination of three more specific concepts. These can be labeled validity, comprehensiveness, and verisimilitude. A simulation game is *valid* if it truly and accurately represents those aspects of the real situation that it is intended to simulate. A game is *comprehensive* if it includes all the important aspects of the real situation and simulates them in sufficient detail. A game has *verisimilitude* if it gives the players a feeling of being in the real situation.

Each of these qualities is important for a different reason. Validity is necessary in order for the game to have any educational value. In fact, a game that is not valid is harmful, as it presents a false and misleading picture of the real situation. Comprehensiveness determines the limits of the educational value of the game; obviously, the game can teach only those aspects of the real situation that are included in the game and can teach only as much information about them as the game contains. Verisimilitude increases the effectiveness of the game by making the game believable. For this reason, it is especially important if the game is intended to change the players' attitudes or values, or if the game is intended to train the players to function in the real situation. (Army war games are the classic example.) In short, the game's validity determines whether what it teaches is true; its comprehensiveness determines how much it teaches; and its verisimilitude determines the effectiveness with which it teaches.

Validity is the one aspect of realism that should never be compromised. In the course of designing and revising a simulation game, you will have to sacrifice both comprehensiveness and verisimilitude for the sake of playability; the only way to avoid these sacrifices would be to place the students directly in the real situation instead of having them play a game. However, if you design a game that is not valid but has considerable comprehensiveness and verisimilitude, you will have produced a grossly misleading learning situation.

The realism of your game can be evaluated only by someone who knows the real situation. For this reason it is a good idea to give the game a trial playing with a group of experts on the real situation, or with a group that contains one or two such experts. (Your "experts" need not be nationally recognized authorities on the subject; other teachers in your subject area can be quite helpful.)

Validity

In judging the validity of your game, you and your "panel of experts" should consider three key questions:

1. Are the *choices of strategy* available to each player the same as those available to the participant in the real situation?

2. Do the *immediate results* of each decision by a player—the rewards or penalties that he experiences as a result of his decision—correspond to those that would result from the same decision in the real situation?

3. Is the *final outcome* of each combination of players' decisions and external factors the same as it would be in the real situation?

If the answer to any of these questions is "no," the next question must be "why not?" In this way you can identify the aspects of your game that may not be valid.

Question 1 is partly a question of comprehensiveness, especially in the case of unusual strategies that seldom occur in real life. Insofar as it is a question of comprehensiveness, a "no" answer may be tolerated. The same can be said of questions 2 and 3, insofar as they concern matters of detail. But all three questions are basically questions of validity. After you have made allowances for the fact that some aspects of the real situation have been left out of the game, the answer to each of the three questions must then be "yes"; otherwise the game is not valid.

Historical games pose special problems of validity, because even the experts may disagree as to what would have been the results of decisions that were never made. (What would have happened, for example, if Japan had not attacked the United States in 1941?) In this case you must choose the interpretation you want your game to teach. You can also construct an alternate version of the game that teaches a different interpretation and have the class play both versions. You may be able to accomplish this change simply by changing the chance devices, that is, by using different dice tables, spinners, or decks of chance cards.

Comprehensiveness

As you increase the comprehensiveness of your simulation game, by including more aspects of the real situation and simulating them in greater detail, you increase the potential educational value of the game; but you also make the game harder to play and harder to learn to play. Some compromise must be made. Your decision will depend on the educational objectives of the game, your students' ability and knowledge of the subject, and the amount of class time you intend to spend on the game. Obviously, a game that takes a week of class time can be more comprehensive than one that takes only twenty minutes. Just as obviously, a world politics game intended for government policy-makers will be more comprehensive than one intended for junior high school students.

There is another consideration that will help determine the comprehensiveness of your game: the amount of time you can afford to spend designing it. As the game becomes more complex, the amount of time and effort necessary to determine all the interactions among the players and external factors increases tremendously.

Fortunately, there is a solution to the problem of comprehensiveness. The solution is to have the game playable at several levels of complexity. The first level is the simplest possible version of the game, one that the players can learn without much difficulty. Higher levels of the game introduce additional aspects of the real situation. By allowing the complexity of your game to vary in this way, you can design a game that is useful with students of widely varying levels of previous knowledge.

There are a number of ways in which you can reduce the complexity of your game. You can reduce the number of roles. (Roles that you remove from the game may become external factors.) You may be able to simplify each player's goals. You may find a simpler way to represent the players' resources. You may simplify the interactions by not permitting the players to use strategies that are never (or almost never) used in the real situation, or by ignoring certain possible but highly improbable results. (However, you should not ignore any possibilities important enough to influence the decisions of the participants in the real situation.) You may be able to combine or remove some steps in the sequence of events. And you may be able to hold constant in the game some external factors that vary in the real situation. To make the game more comprehensive (and, necessarily, more complex), you can reverse any of these procedures.

Verisimilitude

Verisimilitude is difficult to plan for when designing a simulation game. To some extent it is a natural result of the structure of the game, but it is also partly the product of structurally irrelevant details. For example, in a game that simulates the international situation that led to World War I, the countries could be identified as "Country A," "Country B," and so on. Identifying them with real names such as Germany, Russia, France, Austria-Hungary increases the verisimilitude of the game.

The main drawback of verisimilitude is that it may lead the players to engage in role-playing and thus distract their attention from the structure of the game. A player whose country is identified as "Germany" may behave differently from the way he would if his country were identified only as "Country A." For this reason, you may deliberately try to reduce the verisimilitude of your game if your objective is to have your students understand the more abstract relationships that operate in the real situation. If you go too far in reducing the verisimilitude of the game, however, the players may fail to see some of the analogies between the game and the real situation while they are playing the game, and you will have to lead them to discover these analogies by means of a follow-up discussion.

There are many ways to increase the verisimilitude of a game without changing its basic structure. You can have the players take the names of participants in the real situation. You can give each player a "profile" that contains a verbal description of his role in addition to the information he needs in order to play the game. If you have any artistic talent, you can add illustrations to the materials. You can include features on the board that are not necessary for the game (being careful that they do not distract the players from the essential features). You can write messages on the chance cards to explain the results. You can require the players to fill out forms when persons in the real situation would have to do so, as when applying for a job, buying land, making a loan, and so on. You can require the players to use protocol similar to that which would be used in the real situation; for example, in a game that simulates a legislative session, players may be required to address the chairman as "Mr. Speaker." Some of these devices require no extra time or effort from the players or from the game designer; others require a great deal. When you see how your students respond, you will know whether or not the extra effort is worthwhile.

PLAYABILITY

A simulation game is playable if it works well as a game. For a classroom game to be playable, the students must want to play it and they must be able to play it. Therefore, the game must be enjoyable or interesting (or both), and it must be reasonably easy to learn to play and to play correctly. It must also be reasonably easy to administer.

Obviously, the playability of a game depends on the players. A game that is unplayable with one group of students may be playable with a more mature or more intelligent group. Nevertheless, there are some techniques you can use to make your game more playable with any group, and there are some things that you should generally try to avoid if you possibly can.

Do all you can to avoid idle time for the players. When players have to wait too long between moments of participation, they lose interest in the game. This problem is especially acute in classroom games because of the large number of students and because students who lose interest can quickly become disruptive. There is no simple solution to the problem. In games in which several players move in sequence, you can prevent one slow player from holding up the game by including a rule stating that any player who is not ready to take his turn will lose his turn. (Alternatively, the rule may specify a certain move to be made automatically for him.)

Unless your game is designed to provide practice in arithmetic, avoid having the players make complex calculations during the game. These calculations slow the game down and may also produce errors. Fortunately, they can often be avoided by the use of tables and graphs.

Avoid unnecessarily complicated or confusing players' materials and board layouts. You can often make these materials more understandable by the simple device of color-coding, that is, by using the same color for related materials. For example, each player may have his own color, and all materials that he uses will be of that color. Or, each step in the order of play may be indicated by a different color, and all materials used during a certain step will be of the same color. Or, each color may represent a different strategy, and all materials that a player must use if he follows a certain strategy will be of the same color.

Try to avoid rules that are easily misunderstood or likely to be unintentionally violated (for example, a rule that calls for a player to get cards but forbids him to look at them until later). Always state the rules as simply as possible and try to anticipate the players' understandings or misinterpretations. It is a good idea to give the game at least one trial playing with students who are slightly less able than those for whom the game is intended.

ADJUSTING THE PARAMETERS

The parameters in a simulation game are the quantities that are determined by the game designer. They are constant in the sense that they do not vary during the game, but they are variable in the sense that the game designer can change them if he wants to. One type of parameter is the amount of each resource that each player has at the beginning of the game. The numbers in the scoring formulas are another type of parameter. When chance devices are used, the probabilities of the different results are parameters.

Often the parameters are determined (or greatly limited) by the real situation; for example, in a game which simulates economic conditions in the 1960s in the United States, twenty cents per hour would not be a realistic wage. But often the parameters cannot be measured accurately in the real situation, especially when they represent intangibles such as power, prestige, or satisfaction. If the parameters in your game are of this type you will probably have to adjust them by trial and error. To do so, you must give the game several trial playings and examine the strategies used by the players and the resulting outcome of the game. This whole process rests on the assumption that when the *results* of different combinations of players' strategies in the game are the same as they would be in the real situation, the parameters are correct. If the interactions between players are probabilistic and if their probabilities cannot be determined from the real situation, you will have to make the further assumption that when the *players' behavior* in the game corresponds to that of the participants in the real situation, the parameters are correct. These are strong assumptions, but without them you have nothing but intuition to guide you.

SUMMARY

Just as the players of the game often find it useful to have a summary of the rules available, you, the reader and game designer, may find it useful to have a summary of the game-designing process presented in this chapter. Here, then, is an outline of the step-by-step process.

1.   Decide what you want your game to teach.
2.   Select the real-life situation you want your game to simulate.
3.   Design the general structure of your game, considering (roughly in this order):
   a.   roles
   b.   goals
   c.   resources
   d.   interactions
   e.   sequence of events
   f.   external factors
4.   Design the materials for your game, which may include:
   a.   board
   b.   tokens
   c.   score sheets
   d.   tables and graphs
   e.   chance cards, spinners, or dice
5.   Write the rules, answering (in order) each of the following questions:
   a.   What real-life situation does the game simulate?
   b.   What is the object of the game?
   c.   What does each of the materials represent?
   d.   How do you set up the game for playing?
   e.   What is the order of play?
   f.   What do the players do during each step of the order of play?
   g.   How does the game end?
   h.   How might a player play a typical round of the game?
6.   Test and revise the game (adjusting the parameters, if necessary), paying special attention to:
   a.   realism: validity, comprehensiveness, and verisimilitude
   b.   playability

You are now ready to design a simulation game. Design as good a game as you can in the time you are willing to spend, and remember: your game need not be perfect in order to have educational value.

Good luck.

Abt, Clark. 1968. "Games for Learning," in Boocock, Sarane S. and Schild, E. O. (eds.), *Simulation Games in Learning*. Beverly Hills, Calif.: Sage Publications.

5 Research on Games

CLAIMS FOR GAMES

There has been so much literature proclaiming the value of simulation gaming that the editor of *Media and Methods* (October, 1970) was led to remark, tongue in cheek:

Simulation games will revolutionize teaching (what won't?). Students will freak out on them (thus solving the drug problem), low tracks will suddenly become hypermotivated, teachers will become guides (referees, one supposes), and we will lock-step toward Nirvana with a pair of dice in hand.

The sarcasm is not entirely inappropriate. Consider the following list of assertions, all taken from one recent book on simulation (Gordon, 1970, emphasis added):

Games are intrinsically *motivating* because the form is characterized by several dramatic features that are independent of the subject or issues dealt with. [p. 19]

The *sense of efficacy* that games permit and encourage . . . is an important educational benefit. [p. 20]

They [games] can serve as a partial *antidote to the passivity* that the typical school environment tends to create or reinforce. [p. 20]

The player . . . knows the *reason for success or failure.* [p. 21]

Games inject *realism* into learning situations . . . . [p. 23]

Game learning tends to have *closer connections to students' lives* than many conventional classroom activities. [p. 23]

In games, *peer interaction* is harnessed for specific educational goals. [p. 24]

Games tap the human instinct to *cooperate.* [p. 25]

In a game, there is no guarantee that "the best" students will win . . . *Verbal skills*, which are critical in conventional activities, *are often subordinate in games.* [p. 25]

Gordon goes on to argue that games teach factual information, analysis and synthesis, judgment, verbal and interpersonal skills, flexibility, transfer learning, and problem solving and also have socialization effects.[1] The road to Nirvana, no doubt.

By now, you are probably aware of some problems with these claims. We have already pointed out that a game is usually designed to produce one or two of many kinds of learning; no one game can do all things. It should be apparent too that not all games are equally realistic. Nor do they all involve the quick feedback necessary for learning "the reason for success or failure." And games vary in the amount of peer interaction they permit.

Why do we and others continue to state these claims for simulation games? Is there any validity to them? The answer depends partly upon the type of evidence you will accept. There is much anecdotal, subjective data that appear to show that games "do" things. Students *appear* to be motivated; they *appear* to understand the underlying model. These experiences can be dramatic for the observer, as the following example illustrates:

One memorable experience from the testing has had a deep influence upon my thinking about the education of deprived children, as well as the design and presentation of instructional games. One group, consisting of youngsters who were considered all but uneducable by most of their teachers, taught themselves to play the game *Life Career* in one afternoon with no assistance other than a very inadequate set of rules (seven pages long, hastily typed, with a large amount of crossed-out words, misspellings, etc.)! The first half hour, during which these students struggled to work with the awkward, unattractive materials, was painful to observe, but within two hours, all were playing with some degree of facility, had corrected most of their own initial

---

[1] We have not selected a straw man in making this argument. The reader may find similar lists in Raser (1969: 128-29), Boocock and Schild (1968), Abt (1970), and Nesbitt (1971). Also see our own first two chapters in this volume.

mistakes, and, most important, had for the first time shaken off the passivity, aloofness, and faint hostility that had characterized this group.[2]

The events in this case were seen through the eyes of the game designer, who was field-testing the game, certainly a less than objective observer.[3] There are two major problems with this kind of evidence. One is that the observer misperceives what he sees. A teacher may, in seeing a sudden surge of classroom activity, say, "My students are learning more during the game." In fact, the observable activity may have little to do with learning; the class might have learned more by filling in a work sheet. Here the observer's enthusiasm prevents him from critically examining whether class activity and learning are the same thing. Because simulation games generally produce more activity than most other class activities, this kind of error is understandably prevalent.

Second, the observer may make a correct observation and then jump to the conclusion that the simulation is a cause or factor of the observed behavior. For example, an observer may note that attendance is high during a week of simulation activity and conclude that "simulations motivate children to attend school." This conclusion is not reasonable unless the observer has also considered other possible reasons for high attendance that week. A test for cause and effect calls for a comparison of students exposed to the simulation gaming with a similar group of students who were not exposed to it—in other words, for an experimental design.

One problem with some of the research studies on the effectiveness of simulation games, including several studies on games and attitude change, is that the investigators designed their questionnaires without any clear hypothesis in mind. An example is Cohen's (1969) study of attitude change resulting from the *Democracy* and *Consumer* games. Students were surveyed before and after play on such topics as school and politics. There was not always a clear connection between the survey items and the game content. Finding that some attitudes changed while others did not, Cohen concludes that " ... students who had played the game were in the process of acquiring more sophisticated notions as to what is involved in the political process" (p. 16). However, Cohen did not set out specifically to study political sophistication, and her hypothesis was made after the fact. For this reason, her study (like some other studies on attitude change) leaves the reader with the feeling that this investigator would have had an explanation for any results she might have found.

---

[2] Boocock (1972).

[3] For similar anecdotal material, see Inbar and Stoll (1972), Abt (1970), or Carlson (1970).

THE EVIDENCE

Let us look at some of the more systematic studies of simulation in the classroom to see whether their results support the various claims for gaming. Most of the research has focused upon the effects of games upon individual learning. Many of the studies we cite have utilized both experimental and control groups. In most of the studies, the researchers have investigated a few specific hypotheses and attempted to develop measures of the variables that interested them. Rather than review the research study by study, we have organized the findings according to the questions they help to answer. Some studies are cited more than once.

Do Simulation Games Teach Factual Knowledge?

Livingston (1971b) found that high school students who spent five hours playing *Venture* outperformed a control group who received no instruction, on a short test of business facts and concepts.

Cohen (1970) found that junior high school students who played *Consumer* for a week performed better on a test of knowledge of credit terms than did a control group who received no instruction.

Boocock (1966; also reported in Boocock and Coleman, 1966, and in Boocock and Schild, 1968, pp. 107-33) found that, among delegates to a National 4-H Club convention who spent three hours playing either *Life Career* or *Democracy*, the group who played *Life Career* did better on a short test of career-related information.

Anderson (1970) found that twelfth-grade students who played and discussed *Consumer* for six class periods did about as well on a test of factual knowledge about consumer credit as did a control group whose teachers "were instructed to teach ... with conventional techniques that represented their usual style of instruction and to exert their best ability ..." (p. 46).

Heinkel (1970) found that a class of college students who played *NAPOLI* for four hours showed the same amount of "cognitive learning" as a control group taught by a "lecture-question-answer" method; both groups showed substantial increases from pre-test to post-test.

Boocock (1963) found that high school students who played an election campaign game for six class periods made only slight gains on a short test of factual knowledge about politics.

Boocock, Schild, and Stoll (1967) compared high school students who played *Democracy* for three class periods and *Life Career* for five class periods with a control group who, during the same time, "read and discussed materials covering the same content as the two games used in the experimental classes" (p. 7). The control group outperformed the experimental group on the tests used to measure learning from the games.

Garvey and Seiler (1966) compared high school seniors who played an early version of the *Inter-Nation Simulation*, as part of a six-week unit on international relations, with a control group who received "instruction similar in every respect to that received by the experimental group except that simulation periods were replaced by lectures and discussions" (p. 3). The control group made larger gains than the experimental group on a test of factual and conceptual knowledge. When the students were retested two months after the completion of the unit, the control group showed larger gains from pre-test to retention test.

Magnelia (1969) found that high school students showed greater knowledge of international politics after playing the *Inter-Nation Simulation* for a full day. A control group which received no instruction showed no improvement.

Wing (1966; also reported in Boocock and Schild, 1968, pp. 155-165) compared sixth graders who played the computer-based *Sumerian Game* and *Sierra Leone* individually at computer terminals with a control group who studied the same subject matter "by conventional classroom methods, with a teacher considered to be especially talented and creative" (p. 32). The control group received fifteen hours of instruction on each subject; the experimental group required an average of ten hours to complete the *Sumerian Game* and five hours to complete *Sierra Leone*. The experimental group outperformed the control group on the *Sumerian* test; the control group outperformed the experimental group on the *Sierra Leone* test.

Baker (1968) compared two eighth-grade classes who studied a fifteen-day unit in American history by means of a simulation game with two "traditional classes" in which "the teacher presented the historical material stated in the book, each pupil read the material, discussed it briefly in class and was occasionally given some of the questions at the end of the chapter to write out or discuss in class orally" (pp. 138-39). (Baker taught all four classes himself.) The simulation group outperformed the "traditional" group by a substantial margin on a test of factual knowledge given at the end of the unit. When the same test was given again, without notice, six weeks later, the simulation group again outperformed the control group, by a smaller margin.

Johnson and Euler (1971) administered tests of educational and career information to a group of ninth-grade students who played *Life Career* one hour per week for six weeks and a control group who studied an occupational unit consisting of lectures, discussion, and filmstrips. The tests were administered at the end of the six-week period and again four weeks later. On the test of educational information, the control group outperformed the experimental group at the end of the unit, but the two groups performed equally well four weeks

later. On the test of career information, the two groups performed equally well at the end of the unit, but the experimental group outperformed the control group four weeks later.

Do Simulation Games Teach Intellectual Skills?

Fletcher (1968; also reported in Fletcher, 1971) found that fifth-graders improved significantly in their ability to read compass directions on a map after ten plays of *Caribou Hunt*.

Anderson (1970) compared high school seniors who played and discussed *Consumer* for six class periods with a control group who received conventional lessons on consumer credit and finance. He found that "learning to select and sign a credit contract with terms and conditions most favorable to the borrower was learned equally well by the students in each treatment group" (p. 53).

Do Simulation Games Teach Social Skills?

Schild (1966; also reported in Boocock and Schild, 1968, pp. 143-54) compared two groups of college students playing an early version of *Generation Gap*. One group had previously played *Democracy*; the other had not. The students who had played *Democracy* were more successful at resolving conflicts through negotiation when they played *Generation Gap* than the students who had not played *Democracy*.

Kidder and Guthrie (1972) used the game *Modifying* with college students who were learning to teach mentally retarded children. On a performance test of the use of behavior modification techniques with real retarded children, the student teachers who played the game scored higher than a control group who received no treatment, but no higher than a group who listened to a lecture on the use of behavior modification techniques.

Do Simulation Games Change Students' Opinions and Attitudes?[4]

Boocock (1963) found that high school students who spent six class periods playing an election campaign game had more negative attitudes toward politics after the game than before.

Cohen (1969) found that junior high school students who played *Democracy* for a week became less likely to agree that congressmen should vote "the way they believe, even though the voters who elected them may not agree."

Heinkel (1970) found that college students who played *NAPOLI* for four hours showed attitudes toward government that were "more favorable and less unfavorable" but also "more extreme in feelings" than those of a control group taught by conventional methods.

[4] Since this book is about simulation games, we will not attempt to summarize the many research studies on role playing and attitude change. If you are interested in this topic, see Elms (1969).

Livingston (1970a, 1971a), in four separate studies using *Ghetto* with players ranging in age from ninth-grade through adult, found that the players held more favorable opinions about poor people after playing the game but that this effect of the game was temporary.

Livingston (1972) found that, as a result of playing *Democracy* for two class periods, junior high school students who had previously felt that voting agreements between congressmen are unfair, undemocratic, and dishonest no longer held these opinions. In a subsequent study, Livingston and Kidder (1973) found that both the structural elements and the role-taking aspects of the game contributed to this effect.

Boocock (1966; also reported in Boocock and Coleman, 1966, and Boocock and Schild, 1968, pp. 107-33) found that, among high school age delegates to a national 4-H Club convention who played *Life Career* for a single three-hour session, boys who played the role of a potential school dropout became more sympathetic toward the dropout, while girls who played a similar role became less sympathetic.

Baker (1968) found that a "Pre-Civil War Simulation" led eighth graders to express "a more favorable attitude toward centralized and efficient policy-making procedures."

Cherryholmes (1965) used an early version of the *Inter-Nation Simulation* with high school students as "the core activity of a six-week unit in international relations" (p. 227). He found that the students' opinions about foreign policy changed in three ways: They were more likely to favor a "centralized and efficient policy-making procedure," they showed a greater appreciation of the complexity of foreign-policy decision-making, and they acquired "realistic attitudes" toward international relations. "Realistic attitudes" meant disagreeing with such statements as "A democratic country should always follow democratic principles in determining and carrying out its foreign policy" and agreeing that "The United States should form alliances with dictators if this would help stop the spread of world communism" (p. 230).

Garvey and Seiler (1966) compared twelfth-grade students who played the *Inter-Nation Simulation* as part of a six-week unit in international relations with a control group who studied the same unit with lectures and discussions substituted for the simulation sessions. Before and after the unit, both groups answered a 31-question survey of attitudes toward international relations. There was "no identifiable pattern for the differences between the control group and the experimental group" (p. 8).

Lee and O'Leary (1971) found that, among high school students who played the *Inter-Nation Simulation* for three six-hour sessions and discussed it for two one-hour class periods, attitudes toward international relations became more "realistic," but only for those students who initially

scored low on a scale designed to measure "trust in people."

Do Students Prefer Simulation Games to Other Classroom Activities?

Cherryholmes (1965) found that, among high school students who participated in the *Inter-Nation Simulation* as the main activity in a six-week unit, 87 percent agreed that they enjoyed participating in the simulation, while only 3 per cent disagreed.

Boocock (1963) found that, among high school students who participated in an election campaign game for six class periods, 87 per cent thought the game was "more interesting or challenging" than their regular class work.

Cohen (1970) found that, among inner-city junior high school students who played *Consumer* for a week, 93 per cent felt it was more interesting than their regular class work.

Cohen (1969) found that junior high school students who played *Consumer* and *Democracy* as part of a special summer school program for unmotivated students preferred the games to regular class work for several reasons: 87 per cent thought the games were more interesting; 82 per cent thought the games allowed them more freedom to work on their own; 61 per cent thought the games gave them a better idea of how well they were doing.

Edwards (1971b) found that, among junior college students who participated in a business simulation as a regular weekly activity in an introductory business course, 69 per cent agreed that they did more work and were more interested in the course than they would have been without the game.

Robinson et al. (1966) found that when students in college political science classes were assigned at random to simulation (*Inter-Nation*) or case-study sections, 37 per cent of the students in the simulation section said at the end of the course that they preferred case study, while only 24 per cent of the students in the case-study section said they preferred simulation.

Fletcher (1968) found that, among fifth-grade students who played *Caribou Hunt* ten times, 73 per cent agreed that they "would like to play the game lots more times," while only 14 per cent disagreed. In addition, 50 per cent agreed that they "liked playing the games better than anything else we've done in studying the Eskimos," while only 20 per cent disagreed.

Do Simulation Games Motivate Students?

Boocock (1963) found that high school students who had participated in an election campaign game for six class periods read and talked more about local elections than did comparable students who had not participated.

Clarke (1970) used a simulation of a national nominating convention with high school students for three weeks prior to an actual election campaign. A larger percentage of these students participated in the election campaign than did students from a comparable high school at which the simulation was not run.

Livingston (1972) found no significant increase in interest in politics for junior high school students who played *Democracy* for two class periods.

Livingston (1970a) found that twelfth-grade students expressed slightly less interest in learning about the problems of the poor after four class periods of playing *Ghetto* than before.

Livingston (1970b; also reported in Livingston, 1971c) found that junior high school and high school students who played *Trade and Develop* for two class periods expressed no more interest in learning tasks related to the subject of the game and performed no better at them than students who did not play the game.

Robinson *et al.* (1966) compared college political-science students assigned at random to a "simulation section," in which they played the *Inter-Nation Simulation*, with students assigned to a "case section," in which they discussed case studies relevant to the course, and found that attendance was higher at the simulation sessions than at the case-study sessions.

Magnelia (1969) found that high school students' interest in international politics increased after they played the *Inter-Nation Simulation* for a full day. A control group which received no instruction showed no increase in interest.

Cohen (1970) found that when a teacher at an inner-city junior high school used *Consumer* in one of his classes for one week, school attendance increased markedly in that class. There was no corresponding increase in attendance for another comparable class, taught by the same teacher, which did not play the game.

Do Simulation Games Increase Students' Belief in Their Ability to Succeed or to Control Their Environment?

Boocock, Schild, and Stoll (1967) in a study using *Democracy* and *Life Career* reported "no clear evidence that game experience either increases or decreases players' sense of control differently from the more conventional classroom situation." Stoll (1971) later replicated this design with other games and other students, again failing to find that the games contributed to a sense of mastery over the environment.

Boocock (1966; also reported in Boocock and Coleman, 1966, and in Boocock and Schild, 1968, pp. 107-133) found that the *Democracy* game produced a slight increase in the players' feelings of political efficacy, as measured by four questionnaire items.

Livingston (1972) conducted two studies in which junior high school students played *Democracy* for two class periods. The players' feelings of political efficacy, as measured by three questionnaire items, increased in one study but not in the other.

Vogel (1970) compared sixth-grade students who played *City Council* (an adaptation of *Democracy*) for sixteen class periods with a control group who received a unit of instruction based on readings and films and designed to parallel the game as closely as possible. Using a seven-item questionnaire scale to measure feelings of political efficacy before and after the unit, he found that, while the political efficacy scores of the control group increased, those of the experimental group increased by a larger amount.

Edwards (1971b) found that junior college students who participated in a business simulation generally reported that the experience had increased their confidence in their ability to succeed in business, though a substantial minority disagreed. He also found a sizable positive correlation between students' reported increase in self-confidence and their understanding of the simulation game, as measured by an objective test.

Do Simulation Games Provide Special Opportunities for Low-ability and Low-achieving Students?

Boocock and Schild (1968, p. 256) conclude from three unpublished studies that "consistent empirical evidence shows that the relationship between learning in a game situation and performance in the conventional school setting . . . is very weak." This absence of a relationship would imply that a student who performs poorly in conventional classwork is as likely as any other student to do well at learning in a game. Consequently, games should provide a special opportunity for the low achiever.

Edwards (1971b) found that, among junior college students who participated in a business simulation, low-achievers were no more likely than other students to agree that the game had provided them with a special opportunity to show the instructor that they understood the course material.

Braskamp and Hodgetts (1971) found that, among college business students participating in a business simulation, students with low grade-point averages generally outscored students with high grade-point averages. (The criterion was performance in the simulation itself, not on a test.)

Magnelia (1969) found that, among high school students who played the *Inter-Nation Simulation* for a full day, students of high ability showed the largest increase in factual knowledge, while students of low ability showed the largest increase in interest in international politics.

Muhlerin (1971) compared ninth-grade students who played *Life Career* for twelve consecutive days with control groups who "continued their usual classroom activities" and found that the game "increased awareness of factors to consider in curriculum choice, and in the relation of curriculum choice to occupational choice for above average ability students." He reported no such increase for low ability students.

Fletcher (1968, also reported in Fletcher, 1971) conducted a study in which fifth graders played *Caribou Hunt* for several class periods. He found that students who had been judged by their teachers to be of low ability were as good as other students at learning successful strategies within the context of the game. However, these students were much poorer than the others at understanding the analogies between elements of the game and the corresponding elements of the real situation. They were also poorer at perceiving the consequences of the rules of the game and at predicting the effects of possible rule changes in the game.

Edwards (1971a) obtained results similar to Fletcher's in a study in which eighth graders played *Trade and Develop*. Students' ability was weakly related to learning of strategies, somewhat more strongly related to correct perceptions of the game, and still more strongly related to understanding of the analogies between the game and the real situation.

Do Simulation Games Help Students Learn Factual Information from Other Sources?

Livingston (1970b; also reported in Livingston, 1971c) compared eighth- and tenth-grade students who had played *Trade and Develop* for two class periods with control groups who had not, on tasks requiring the students to learn facts about international trade from a textbook and a filmstrip. There were no differences between experimental and control groups in learning, in any of three similar experiments.

Do Simulation Games Teach Critical Thinking?

Garvey and Seiler (1966) found that twelfth graders who played the *Inter-Nation Simulation* as part of a six-week unit performed no better on two critical-thinking tests than students who studied the same unit with lectures and discussions in place of the simulations.

Do Simulation Games Increase Students' Tolerance for Ambiguity?

Lee and O'Leary (1971) compared high school students who played the *Inter-Nation Simulation* for three six-hour sessions and discussed it for two one-hour class periods, with a control group who spent the same amount of time studying international relations by participating in debates and panel discussions and writing research papers. Both groups were tested immediately before the experiment and tested again four weeks after the experiment. Students in the experimental group increased in tolerance for ambiguity, while those in the control group did not.

CONCLUSIONS

In the preceding section, we have tried to present the evidence on each question as fairly as we can. Nevertheless, there are probably some relevant research studies that have escaped our attention. We also realize that our own biases are reflected in our selection, organization, and reporting of the findings. Therefore, we want to emphasize that the following conclusions are not the final word. Rather, they represent the best answer we can give to the question, "What does the existing research show about the effectiveness of simulation games for teaching social studies?" Here, then, are our conclusions:

1. For teaching factual knowledge and intellectual skills, games generally seem to be about as effective as conventional methods of instruction.

2. Simulation games can often change students' attitudes and opinions. The most common types of attitude change are greater "realism" and greater approval of the real-life persons whose role the students play in the game.

3. Most students prefer simulation games to conventional classroom activities.

4. Students of low academic ability or achievement usually do much better at learning *to play* a simulation game than at learning *from* the game; their greatest difficulty is in transferring their understanding of the game to the real situation that the game represents.

Of course, this short list will grow as more research is done. Some of the studies described earlier in this chapter need to be replicated with different games and different students before their findings can be accepted as generally true. Very little research has been done on the characteristics of a game which may make it more or less effective for achieving certain objectives[5] or on the things a teacher can do to make a game more or less effective.[6] And there has been no systematic research to find out what students learn from designing their own simulation games. When researchers begin to investigate these topics, their results will be of real value to classroom teachers. Until then, you will have to rely on your colleagues' advice and your own experience and judgment.

[5] For one example of this type of research, see Livingston and Kidder (1973).

[6] A preliminary result along this line is Edwards' (1971b) finding that college students who understood the instructor's reasons for using a semester-long business simulation game were more likely to accept the use of game performance as a basis for grading and to agree that the game increased their motivation and self-confidence.

REFERENCES

Abt, Clark. 1970. *Serious Games*. New York: Viking.

Anderson, C. Raymond. 1970. "An Experiment on Behavioral Learning in a Consumer Credit Game." *Simulation and Games* 1: 43-54.

Baker, Eugene H. 1968. "A Pre-Civil War Simulation for Teaching American History." In Boocock, Sarane S., and Schild, E. O. (eds.), *Simulation Games in Learning*. Beverly Hills, Calif.: Sage Publications.

Boocock, Sarane S. 1963. "Effects of Election Campaign Game in Four High School Classes." *Research Program in the Effects of Games with Simulated Environments in Secondary Education. Report No. 1*. Baltimore: Department of Social Relations, Johns Hopkins University.

——. 1966. "An Experimental Study of the Learning Effects of Two Games with Simulated Environments," *American Behavioral Scientist* 10: 8-17.

——. 1972. "A Research and Development Chronicle: The Life Career Game." In Inbar, Michael, and Stoll, Clarice S. (eds.), *Simulation and Gaming in Social Science*. New York: Free Press.

——, and Coleman, James S. 1966. "Games with Simulated Environments in Learning." *Sociology of Education* 39: 215-36.

——, and Schild, E. O. 1968. *Simulation Games in Learning*, Beverly Hills, Calif.: Sage Publications.

——, Schild, E. O., and Stoll, Clarice S. 1967. "Simulation Games and Control Beliefs." Baltimore: Center for Social Organization of Schools, Johns Hopkins University. Report No. 10.

Braskamp, Larry A., and Hodgetts, Richard M. 1971. "The Role of an Objective Evaluation Model in Simulation Gaming." *Simulation and Games* 2: 197-212.

Carlson, Eliot. 1969. *Learning Through Games*. Washington, D.C.: Public Affairs Press.

Cherryholmes, Cleo. 1965. "Developments in Simulation of International Relations for High School Teaching." *Phi Delta Kappan* 46: 227-31.

Clarke, Wentworth. 1970. "A Research Note on Simulation in the Social Sciences." *Simulation and Games* 1: 203-10.

Cohen, Karen. 1969. "The Effects of Two Simulation Games on the Opinions and Attitudes of Selected Sixth, Seventh, and Eighth Grade Students." Baltimore: Center for Social Organization of Schools, Johns Hopkins University. Report No. 42.

——. 1970. "Effects of the Consumer Game on Learning and Attitudes of Selected Seventh Grade Students in a Target-area School." Baltimore: Center for Social Organization of Schools, Johns Hopkins University. Report No. 65.

Edwards, Keith J. 1971a. "The Effect of Ability, Achievement, and Number of Plays on Learning from a Simulation Game. Baltimore: Center for Social Organization of Schools, Johns Hopkins University. Report No. 115.

——. 1971b. "Student Evaluations of a Business Simulation Game as a Learning Experience." Baltimore: Center for Social Organization of Schools, Johns Hopkins University, Report No. 121.

Elms, Alan C. 1969. *Role Playing, Reward, and Attitude Change*. New York: Van Nostrand Reinhold.

Fletcher, Jerry L. 1968. *The Effects of Two Elementary School Social Studies Games: An Experimental Field Study*. Unpublished doctoral dissertation, Harvard University.

——. 1971. "Evaluation of Learning in Two Social Studies Simulation Games." *Simulation and Games* 2: 259-86.

Garvey, Dale M., and Seiler, William H. 1966. "A Study of Effectiveness of Different Methods of Teaching International Relations to High School Students." Unpublished manuscript. Kansas State Teachers College, Emporia, Kansas.

Gordon, Alice Kaplan. 1970. *Games for Growth*. Palo Alto, Calif.: Science Research Associates.

Heinkel, Otto A. 1970. "Evaluation of Simulation as a Teaching Device." *Journal of Experimental Education* 38 (3):32-36.

Inbar, Michael, and Stoll, Clarice S. 1972. *Simulation and Gaming in Social Science*. New York: Free Press.

Johnson, Richard H., and Euler, Delores E. 1971. "Effects of the Life Career Game on Learning and Retention of Educational-Occupational Information Among Ninth Graders." Unpublished manuscript. Department of Counselor Education, University of Florida, Gainesville, Florida.

Kidder, Steven J., and Guthrie, John T. 1972. "The Training Effects of a Behavior Modification Game." *Simulation and Games* 3: 17-28.

Lee, Robert S., and O'Leary, Arlene. 1971. "Attitude and Personality Effects of a Three-Day Simulation." *Simulation and Games* 2: 309-47.

Livingston, Samuel A. 1970a. "Simulation Games and Attitude Change: Attitudes Toward the Poor." Baltimore: Center for Social Organization of Schools, Johns Hopkins University. Report No. 63.

——. 1970b. "Simulation Games as Advance Organizers in the Learning of Social Science Materials: Experiments 1-3." Baltimore: Center for Social Organization of Schools, Johns Hopkins University. Report No. 64.

——. 1971a. "Simulation Games and Attitudes Toward the Poor: Three Questionnaire Studies." Baltimore: Center for Social Organization of Schools, Johns Hopkins University. Report No. 118.

——. 1971b. "Two Types of Learning in a Business Simulation." Baltimore: Center for Social Organization of Schools, Johns Hopkins University. Report No. 104.

——. 1971c. "Will a Simulation Game Improve Student Learning of Related Factual Material?" *Educational Technology* 11: 19-20.

——. 1972. "Effects of a Legislative Simulation Game on the Political Attitudes of Junior High School Students." *Simulation and Games* 3: 41-51.

—— and Kidder, Steven J. 1973. Role Identification and Game Structure: Effects on Political Attitudes. *Simulation and Games*, 4(1) (in press).

Magnelia, Paul F. 1969. "The Inter-Nation Simulation and Secondary Education." *Journal of Creative Behavior* 3: 115-21.

Muhlerin, Brian Clyde. 1971. *The Effects of Simulated Career Planning on the Vocational Maturity of Ninth Grade Youth*. Unpublished doctoral dissertation, University of Maine at Orono. Abstract.

Nesbitt, William. 1971. *Simulation Games for the Social Studies Classroom*. New York: Foreign Policy Association.

Raser, John R. 1969. *Simulation and Society*. Boston: Allyn and Bacon.

Robinson, James A., Anderson, Lee F., Herrmann, Margaret G., and Snyder, Richard C. 1966. "Teaching with Inter-Nation Simulation and Case Studies." *American Political Science Review* 60: 53-66.

Schild, E. O. 1966. "The Shaping of Strategies." *American Behavioral Scientist* 10: 1-4

Stoll, Clarice S. 1971. "Studies of the Effects of Simulation Gaming on Players' Control Beliefs." Unpublished manuscript. Department of Sociology, Sonoma State College, Rohnert Park, California.

Vogel, Rex W. 1970. "The Effect of a Simulation Game on the Attitude of Political Efficacy of Sixth Grade Students." Master's Thesis, Department of Elementary Education, University of Alberta, Edmonton, Alberta.

Wing, Richard L. 1966. "Two Computer-based Economics Games for Sixth-Graders." *American Behavioral Scientist* 10: 31-34.

Appendix

PUBLISHERS OF SIMULATION GAMES

The following list includes the publishers of simulation games and game-like materials mentioned in the preceding chapters. Some of these publishers also publish other simulation games in addition to those mentioned.

Life Career, Ghetto, Democracy, Consumer, and *Generation Gap* are available from Western Publishing Company, Inc., School and Library Department, 150 Parish Drive, Wayne, New Jersey 07470.

SIMSOC is published by The Free Press, 866 Third Avenue, New York, N. Y. 10022.

Diplomacy is published by Games Research, Inc., 48 Wareham Street, Boston, Mass. 02118.

The Road Game is published by Herder and Herder, 232 Madison Avenue, New York, N. Y. 10016.

The Sumerian Game and *The Sierra Leone Development Game* (both of which require the use of a computer) are available from Board of Co-operative Educational Services, 845 Fox Meadow Road, Yorktown Heights, N. Y. 10598.

Trade and Develop is available from Academic Games Associates, Inc., 430 East 33rd Street, Baltimore, Md. 21218.

Modifying is one of a series of five games in the game kit entitled *Classroom*. For further information contact Academic Games Associates, Inc., 430 East 33rd St., Baltimore, Md. 21218.

Venture was published by The Proctor & Gamble Company, Division of Educational Services, but is no longer available.

The *Inter-Nation Simulation* is published by Science Research Associates, Inc., 259 East Erie Street, Chicago, Ill. 60611.

Caribou Hunt is currently available only as part of a complete one-year social studies curriculum entitled *Man: A Course of Study*, published by Education Development Center, Inc., 15 Mifflin Place, Cambridge, Mass. 02138.

NAPOLI is published by Simile II, 1150 Silverado, La Jolla, California 92037.

Some of the other publishers of simulation games for social studies classes are the following:

Abt Associates, Inc., 55 Wheeler Street, Cambridge, Mass. 02138.

Changing Times Education Service, 1729 H Street, N. W., Washington, D. C. 20006.

High School Geography Project, The Macmillan Company, School Division, 866 Third Avenue, New York, N. Y. 10022. (Note: HSGP materials are complete curriculum units, some of which include simulation games.)

Instructional Simulations, Inc., Box 212, Newport, Minn. 55055.

Interact, P.O. Box 262, Lakeside, Calif. 92040.

KDI Instructional Systems, 1810 MacKenzie Drive, Columbus, Ohio 43220.

Scott, Foresman, and Company, 1900 East Lake Street, Glenview, Ill. 60025.

URBANDYNE, 5659 South Woodlawn Avenue, Chicago, Ill., 60637.

SUGGESTIONS FOR FURTHER READING

Abt, Clark, *Serious Games.* New York: Viking, 1970.
> Although most of the material is limited to games produced by Abt's own company, the volume is readable and valuable for its anecdotal discussions of games in operation.

Boocock, Sarane S., and E. O. Schild (editors). *Simulation Games in Learning.* Beverly Hills, Calif.: Sage, 1968.
> A collection of papers (some previously published, others not) presenting the theory of games as instructional devices and describing some of the early evaluation studies of games.

Carlson, Eliot. *Learning Through Games.* Washington, D.C.: Public Affairs Press, 1969.
> A well-written history and documentary of classroom games—a good book to suggest to curious parents and laymen.

Gordon, Alice Kaplan. *Games for Growth*, Palo Alto, Calif.: Science Research Associates, 1970.

A general introduction, containing a chapter in which the author describes, step by step, how she designed one of her games. One sample "game" included at the end of the volume is really a scenario for a role playing exercise. (See our Chapter 1 for the difference.)

Inbar, Michael, and Clarice S. Stoll. *Simulation Gaming in Social Science*. New York: The Free Press, 1971.
Discusses the design of games and includes case studies by the designers of *Consumer, Life Career, SIMSOC*, and other simulation games. Covers simulation for research and theory-building as well as teaching.

Nesbitt, William A. *Simulation Games for the Social Studies Classroom*. New York: Foreign Policy Association, 1971.
A very brief introduction for the classroom teacher, with emphasis on simulations for teaching foreign policy and international relations.

Raser, John R. *Simulation and Society*. Boston: Allyn and Bacon, 1969.
Weak with regard to classroom games, but a useful introduction to some of the other uses of simulation in social science.

Simulation Gaming News. Box 8899, Stanford University, Stanford, Ca. A bi-monthly newspaper on the latest ideas in simulation gaming, which includes several complete games in every issue. $4.00 annual subscription.

Zuckerman, David W., and Robert E. Horn, *The Guide to Simulations/Games for Education and Training*. Cambridge, Mass.: Information Resources, 1973.
Contains brief descriptions of over 600 games for social studies classes at all levels, preschool through graduate school.

THE INNER-CITY HOUSING GAME

INTRODUCTION

The Inner-City Housing Game is a simulation game for 6 to 10 players. If the players double up, two players to a role, the game can accommodate up to twenty players.

The educational purpose of the game is to familiarize the players with some of the housing problems of the inner city. (Note: Many problems have been deliberately omitted in order to simplify the game, and there are undoubtedly others the author is unaware of.) Specifically, after playing the Inner-City Housing Game, the players should be aware of the following general conditions and relationships:

1. Rents in the inner city are limited by the tenants' ability to pay.
2. Maintenance costs for inner city housing are high.
3. Landlords suffer heavily from vandalism and theft when dwellings are vacant.
4. Damage to rented houses or apartments is often caused by the tenant's children.
5. Housing code enforcement through the criminal courts is always slow and often ineffective.
6. City inspections almost always cause the landlord to be cited for violations in addition to the problem that led the tenant to request an inspection.
7. The housing code violations that are hardest on the tenants are *not* always the ones that cost the most money to correct.

Teachers planning to use the game in class should allow enough time for the students to play it at least twice, and preferably three times, to give each student the chance to be both landlord and tenant. Three or four class periods should provide a good game experience. During the first period the students can learn the game and play one or two practice rounds. In the second period, the students should begin a new game and play as long as there is time (allowing five minutes at the end for cleanup). In the third and fourth periods they should begin a new game each period, changing roles to give every player a chance to be a landlord. In these later games, they should use the optional rules for city inspections.

The problems and costs associated with inner-city housing and the laws governing landlord-tenant relationships vary from city to city; therefore the conditions represented in the game may not be accurate for your city. If this is the case, feel free to make the necessary changes in the rules or the numbers on the cards. For example, if your city has rent controls or a rent-escrow law you may want to include it in the game. Just be sure that the changes you make are based on correct information.

I could not have developed this game without the help of several knowledgeable people who gave freely of their time and expert knowledge. I could not list them all here, but a few deserve special mention: James Bradsher, of Self-Help Housing; Ann Chase, of the Baltimore Department of Social Services; John W. Douglass, of the Maryland House of Delegates; Christopher Hartman, of the Citizens' Planning and Housing Association; William Koons, of the Baltimore Property Owners Association; and Gail Fennessey, of Academic Games Associates. However, none of these people should be considered in any way responsible for any inaccuracies the game may contain.

Samuel A. Livingston

RULES

Object of the Game

There are two kinds of players—landlords and tenants. The landlord's goal is to make as much money as possible. The tenant's goal is to get as many points as possible. The points that the tenant gets represent the value of providing shelter for himself and his family. At the end of the game there will be two winners: the landlord with the most money and the tenant with the most points.

Order of Play

Each round of the game represents one month of real time. Each month follows this sequence of events:

1. Tenants receive income and pay expenses. (Draw chance card first.)

Number of players	Landlords	Tenants	Banker
6	2	3	1
7	2	4	1
8	3	4	1
9	3	5	1
10	3	6	1

Each tenant receives a *tenant* card and a *profile* card. Each landlord receives an *expense* card and $189 in cash. The rest of the money goes into the bank. The *house* cards—one for each landlord—are placed in the center of the table. The banker receives a copy of the rules and the *Housing Court judge's instructions.*

Each house is divided into two apartments. The game begins with all apartments vacant. A landlord may rent an apartment to any tenant for any rent the two can agree on. When a tenant has rented an apartment, he puts his tenant card on the landlord's house card, to show where he is living. Two tenant families may *not* share the same apartment. There is a five-minute time limit for finding apartments. Any apartment that is not rented stays vacant for the first month, and any tenant who does not have an apartment must spend the first month living with relatives. In this case, he keeps his tenant card.

Tenants' Income and Expenses

Each tenant first draws a *chance* card and reads it aloud to the group. This card may affect the amount of money he will receive or the amount he will have to pay for expenses. He then collects his monthly income from the banker and pays back to the banker his monthly expenses (not including rent). These amounts are listed on the tenant's profile card (although they may be affected by the chance card he has drawn).

Note: The tenant should not pay his rent until he has decided whether or not he is going to move.

2. Moving.
3. Rent collection.
4. Eviction.
5. Landlords pay expenses.
6. Wear and tear.
7. City inspections and housing court trials.
8. Tenants' point score.
9. Rent changes. (Landlords may give tenants notice to quit.)

Each step in the order of play must be completed for all players before the next step is begun.

To Start

Divide the players into landlords, tenants, and banker, according to the following table:

Moving

The banker flips a coin once for each tenant, to let the tenant know how much it will cost him to move this month.

Heads: A friend with a car will help you move if you rent a trailer. Expenses $10.

Tails: No help. You have to get a mover. Expenses $90.

A tenant who wants to move must then find an apartment and come to an agreement with the landlord about the rent. Then he pays his moving expenses to the bank and moves his tenant card to the house where he will be living. If he will be living with relatives, he keeps his tenant card.

Rent Collection

A tenant who is renting an apartment pays his rent directly to the landlord. If the tenant does not have the money to pay the rent, or if he feels he cannot afford to pay the rent, he can ask the landlord to accept less than the full amount. If the landlord is not willing to accept less than the full amount, the landlord may pay the bank $3 for a *rent notice* that requires the tenant to pay all the rent he owes next month or be evicted.

Exception: During the last round of the game, the tenant *must* pay the full rent or move out.

Eviction

If a tenant has ignored a rent notice, the landlord must wait one month before evicting him.

If the tenant then does not pay all the rent he owes, the landlord may evict him by paying the bank $35 to cover the cost of moving the tenant's furniture out into the street.

If a tenant has ignored a *60-day notice to quit* (see "Rent Changes") and two months have passed since the landlord gave the tenant the notice, the landlord may evict the tenant by paying the bank $35 to cover the cost of moving the tenant's furniture out into the street.

As soon as a tenant has been evicted, he must move. First he must pay his moving expenses to the bank. If he does not have enough money, he pays the bank all the money he has. Then he must either find an apartment or move in with relatives (in which case he keeps his tenant card).

Landlords' Expenses

Each month the landlord must pay the bank the expenses indicated on his house card. If the landlord does not have enough money to pay his expenses, he may borrow from the bank. For each $100 that he borrows, he must pay back $110 at the end of the game.

Wear-and-Tear

Each tenant who is renting an apartment draws a *wear-and-tear* card and reads it aloud to the group. (Tenants in House No. 1 read their cards first, those in No. 2 second, and so on.) This card tells whether any repairs to the house are necessary. It also tells what will happen if the repairs are not made. Unless the card says otherwise, the information applies only to the apartment of the tenant who draws the card. Repairs to the apartment are the landlord's responsibility, unless the tenant caused the damage. If the landlord decides to make the repairs, he pays the correct amount of money to the bank and puts the card back in the pile. If the landlord refuses to make the repairs, the tenant can pay for them himself if he wants to and if he has the money. The players have two minutes to decide whether to make the repairs and who will pay for them. If nobody has paid for the repairs at the end of the two minutes, the wear-and-tear card stays with the house.

At this time, any landlord who has a vacant apartment must draw a *vacancy* card. This card will indicate repairs that are necessary as a result of vandalism. The vacancy card stays with the apartment until the repairs are made.

If *both* the apartments are vacant, the landlord must draw a *house-empty* card, instead of two vacancy cards for those apartments. Damages listed on this card apply to both apartments. If the house already has a house-empty card, the landlord does not have to draw another one.

If a wear-and-tear card or a vacancy card lists the same kind of damage as a card that is already with the apartment, the card showing the lower cost of repairs should be returned to the deck.

City Inspections and Housing Court Trials

Whenever a landlord refuses to make repairs, the tenant may request a city inspection. The landlord must then draw a *city inspection* card and put it with the house. This card lists the number of additional violations discovered by the inspector and the cost of correcting them.

The landlord then has three months to pay for the repairs listed on both the wear-and-tear card and the city inspection card. Otherwise he goes on trial in Housing Court. The banker acts as judge and conducts the trial according to the Judge's Instructions. He announces the fine the landlord must pay. The landlord must pay the fine immediately (to the bank). He then has another three months to make the repairs or go on trial again.

Tenant's Point Score

The banker writes each tenant's score for the month on the score sheet. The number of points the tenant gets depends on where he is living. The number that goes on the score sheet is the amount shown on the tenant card, minus any points the tenant loses because of wear-and-tear cards or vacancy cards that are still with the house. This number—the amount left after the subtraction—is the tenant's score for the month.

Rent Changes

Whenever an apartment is vacant, the landlord can rent it to a tenant for any rent they can agree on. After the tenant has moved in, the landlord cannot raise the rent unless the tenant either moves out or agrees to let the landlord raise the rent. However, the landlord can terminate the tenant's lease without giving any reason, if he gives the tenant a *60-day notice to quit* two months in advance. The tenant then must move out in two months or be evicted.

Ending the Game

The game can last for any number of rounds. The players can agree in advance whether to play for a certain length of time or a certain number of rounds. The last round ends after the tenants have received their monthly income. The final scores are figured as follows (space is provided on the score sheet for all calculations):

Tenants. Add up your points for all the rounds that have been played. Then add one point for each dollar you have left. This gives you your unadjusted score. Now add up all the points from wear-and-tear cards and vacancy cards that belong to the apartment you are living in. Multiply this number by 10 and subtract that amount from your unadjusted score, to get your actual score. If you are living with relatives, subtract 200 points from your unadjusted score to get your actual score.

Landlords. Count your money. Subtract the amount you owe to the bank ($110 for every $100 you borrowed). This gives your unadjusted score. Now look at the wear-and-tear, vacancy, and empty-house cards that are with your house. Subtract the sum of the cost of repairs listed on these cards from your unadjusted score. But first look in the upper right corner of each card. If the figure ½ is there, you should subtract only half the cost of repairs given on that card. If the number 2 appears, subtract twice the cost of repairs given on that card. After you have subtracted the proper amount for all the cards, you have your actual score.

Some Frequently Asked Questions About the Rules

Q. Can tenants borrow money from the bank?
A. No.

Q. Can tenants borrow money from other tenants?
A. Yes.

Q. Can two tenant families share an apartment?
A. No.

Q. Can the landlord and tenant share the cost of repairs to the house?
A. Yes.

Q. What if a tenant requests an inspection and then moves out?
A. The house gets inspected anyway, and the landlord must take a city inspection card.

Q. If both apartments in a house are empty, does the landlord take two vacancy cards and a house-empty card?

A. No. Just the house-empty card.

Q. Does a vacancy card apply to both apartments?
A. No.

Q. Does a house-empty card apply to both apartments?
A. Yes.

Q. If the landlord gives the tenant a notice to quit, can the tenant just stop paying the rent?
A. Yes, but if he does, he may be evicted after just one month instead of two.

Q. If a tenant moves from one apartment to another apartment in the same house, does he have to pay moving expenses?
A. No.

Q. If a tenant moves out of an apartment and goes to live with relatives, does he have to pay moving expenses?
A. Yes.

Q. If a tenant who has been living with relatives moves to an apartment, does he have to pay moving expenses?
A. Yes.

HOUSING-COURT JUDGE'S INSTRUCTIONS

Look at the number of violations on the city inspection card. Find out if the landlord has repaired the problem that led the tenant to ask for the inspection in the first place. (Is the wear-and-tear card still with the house?) Then flip a coin to determine which of the following lists to read for the amount of the fine.

	Original problem repaired		Original problem not repaired	
	Heads	Tails	Heads	Tails
0 to 4 additional violations	$15	$45	$25	$55
5 to 9 additional violations	$85	$55	$105	$65
10 or more additional violations	$105	$125	$125	$155

Note: The game should also contain play money, about thirty bills in each of the following denominations: 1, 5, 10, 20, 50, 100.

$1	$1	$1
$1	$1	$1
$1	$1	$1
$1	$1	$1
$1	$1	$1

$1	$1	$1
$1	$1	$1
$1	$1	$1
$1	$1	$1
$1	$1	$1

$5	$5	$5
$5	$5	$5
$5	$5	$5
$5	$5	$5
$5	$5	$5

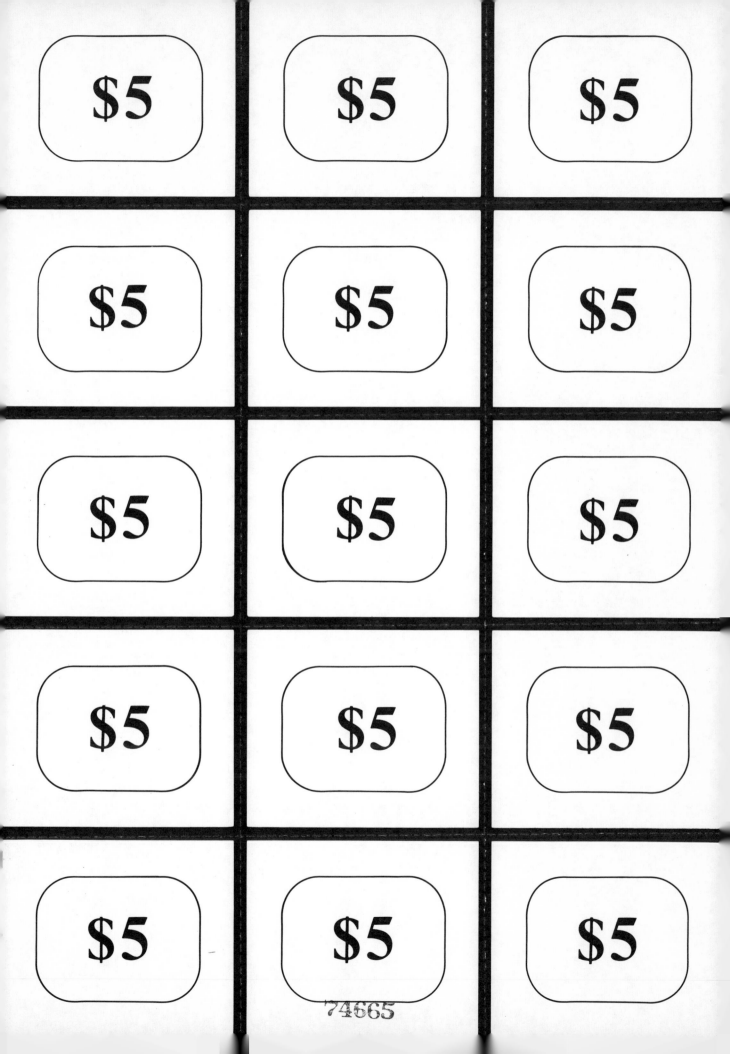

$10	$10	$10
$10	$10	$10
$10	$10	$10
$10	$10	$10
$10	$10	$10

$10	$10	$10
$10	$10	$10
$10	$10	$10
$10	$10	$10
$10	$10	$10

$20	$20	$20
$20	$20	$20
$20	$20	$20
$20	$20	$20
$20	$20	$20

$20	$20	$20
$20	$20	$20
$20	$20	$20
$20	$20	$20
$20	$20	$20

$50	$50	$50
$50	$50	$50
$50	$50	$50
$50	$50	$50
$50	$50	$50

$50	$50	$50
$50	$50	$50
$50	$50	$50
$50	$50	$50
$50	$50	$50

$100	$100	$100
$100	$100	$100
$100	$100	$100
$100	$100	$100
$100	$100	$100

$100	$100	$100
$100	$100	$100
$100	$100	$100
$100	$100	$100
$100	$100	$100

House No. 2

House No. 1

LANDLORD'S EXPENSES
House No. 4

(Total for both apartments, not including maintenance.)

Property tax	$15 per month
Fire insurance	$4 per month
Liability insurance	$4 per month
Management expenses*	$10 per month
Heat*	$25 per month
Water and sewage*	$1 per month for each person living in the house

*These do not have to be paid if both apartments are vacant.
Note: Maintenance expenses will be indicated by Wear-and-Tear cards.

ORDER OF PLAY

1. Tenants receive income and pay expenses (first drawing chance card).

2. Moving.

3. Rent collection.

4. Eviction.

5. Landlords pay expenses.

6. Wear and tear.

7. City inspections and Housing Court trials.

8. Tenants' point score.

9. Rent changes—landlord may terminate lease and give 60 days' notice to quit.

LANDLORD'S EXPENSES
House No. 3

(Total for both apartments, not including maintenance.)

Property tax	$15 per month
Fire insurance	$4 per month
Liability insurance	$4 per month
Management expenses*	$10 per month
Heat*	$25 per month
Water and sewage*	$1 per month for each person living in the house

*These do not have to be paid if both apartments are vacant.
Note: Maintenance expenses will be indicated by Wear-and-Tear cards.

ORDER OF PLAY

1. Tenants receive income and pay expenses (first drawing chance card).

2. Moving.

3. Rent collection.

4. Eviction.

5. Landlords pay expenses.

6. Wear and tear.

7. City inspections and Housing Court trials.

8. Tenants' point score.

9. Rent changes—landlord may terminate lease and give 60 days' notice to quit.

TENANT'S PROFILE

Mr. & Mrs. Pierce—family of 2

Source of income: pension, Social Security.

Monthly income: $220

Monthly expenses, not including rent:
$150 if renting an apartment.
$180 if living with relatives.

Monthly basic score:
50 points if renting an apartment.
No points if living with relatives.

ORDER OF PLAY

1. Tenants receive income and pay expenses (first drawing chance card).

2. Moving.

3. Rent collection.

4. Eviction.

5. Landlords pay expenses.

6. Wear and tear.

7. City inspections and Housing Court trials.

8. Tenants' point score.

9. Rent changes—landlord may terminate lease and give 60 days' notice to quit.

TENANT'S PROFILE

Mr. & Mrs. Jackson—family of 10

Source of income: Mr. Jackson is a factory worker.

Monthly income: $400

Monthly expenses, not including rent:
$320 if renting an apartment.
$360 if living with relatives.

Monthly basic score:
50 points if renting an apartment.
No points if living with relatives.

ORDER OF PLAY

1. Tenants receive income and pay expenses (first drawing chance card).

2. Moving.

3. Rent collection.

4. Eviction.

5. Landlords pay expenses.

6. Wear and tear.

7. City inspections and Housing Court trials.

8. Tenants' point score.

9. Rent changes—landlord may terminate lease and give 60 days' notice to quit.

TENANT'S PROFILE

Mrs. Grant—family of 6

Source of income: husband's Army allotment and part-time work doing laundry and ironing.

Monthly income: $250

Monthly expenses, not including rent:
$175 if renting an apartment.
$210 if living with relatives.

Monthly basic score:
50 points if renting an apartment.
No points if living with relatives.

ORDER OF PLAY

1. Tenants receive income and pay expenses (first drawing chance card).

2. Moving.

3. Rent collection.

4. Eviction.

5. Landlords pay expenses.

6. Wear and tear.

7. City inspections and Housing Court trials.

8. Tenants' point score.

9. Rent changes—landlord may terminate lease and give 60 days' notice to quit.

TENANT'S PROFILE

Mrs. Washington—family of 7

Source of income: works as cleaning woman.

Monthly income: $280

Monthly expenses, not including rent:
$200 if renting an apartment.
$240 if living with relatives.

Monthly basic score:
50 points if renting an apartment.
No points if living with relatives.

ORDER OF PLAY

1. Tenants receive income and pay expenses (first drawing chance card).

2. Moving.

3. Rent collection.

4. Eviction.

5. Landlords pay expenses.

6. Wear and tear.

7. City inspections and Housing Court trials.

8. Tenants' point score.

9. Rent changes—landlord may terminate lease and give 60 days' notice to quit.

TENANT'S PROFILE

Mrs. Adams—family of 7

Source of income: AFDC (Aid to Dependent Children, i.e., welfare).

Monthly income: $240

Monthly expenses, not including rent:
$175 if renting an apartment.
$200 if living with relatives.

Monthly basic score:
60 points if renting an apartment.
No points if living with relatives.

ORDER OF PLAY

1. Tenants receive income and pay expenses (first drawing chance card).

2. Moving.

3. Rent collection.

4. Eviction.

5. Landlords pay expenses.

6. Wear and tear.

7. City inspections and Housing Court trials.

8. Tenants' point score.

9. Rent changes—landlord may terminate lease and give 60 days' notice to quit.

TENANT'S PROFILE

Mr. & Mrs. Hayes—family of 8

Source of income: Mr. Hayes works in a warehouse.

Monthly income: $360

Monthly expenses, not including rent:
$280 if renting an apartment.
$320 if living with relatives.

Monthly basic score:
50 points if renting an apartment.
No points if living with relatives.

ORDER OF PLAY

1. Tenants receive income and pay expenses (first drawing chance card).

2. Moving.

3. Rent collection.

4. Eviction.

5. Landlords pay expenses.

6. Wear and tear.

7. City inspections and Housing Court trials.

8. Tenants' point score.

9. Rent changes—landlord may terminate lease and give 60 days' notice to quit.

HOUSE
No. 1

**LOWER
APARTMENT**

**UPPER
APARTMENT**

HOUSE
No. 2

**LOWER
APARTMENT**

**UPPER
APARTMENT**

HOUSE
No. 3

LOWER
APARTMENT

UPPER
APARTMENT

HOUSE
No. 4

LOWER
APARTMENT

UPPER
APARTMENT

NOTICE TO QUIT

DATE _____

M_____ , Tenant(s)

The undersigned landlord, desirous to have again and repossess the premises known

as _____ in _____ , Anystate, which you

now hold as tenant(s), hereby gives you notice to remove from and quit the same at the end

of your tenancy, which will expire on _____ .

_____

Landlord

_____

Address

NOTICE TO QUIT

DATE _____

M_____ , Tenant(s)

The undersigned landlord, desirous to have again and repossess the premises known

as _____ in _____ , Anystate, which you

now hold as tenant(s), hereby gives you notice to remove from and quit the same at the end

of your tenancy, which will expire on _____ .

_____

Landlord

_____

Address

RENT NOTICE

DISTRICT COURT OF ANYSTATE FOR THE COUNTY OF URBANIA

Whereas _____ , Lessor by _____ .
his duly qualified Agent or Attorney, has this day filed his written complaint in this court,
praying to have again and repossess the premises in said city known as

No. _____ street
rented from him by _____ , Tenant
alleging there is rent due and unpaid to said Lessor the sum of
_____ dollars, _____ cents.

And that by warrant Lessor may have and again repossess the said premises, together with
judgement for the amount of rent due and costs. Wherefore you are hereby ordered to forth-
with summon and notify said tenant to personally appear before JUSTIN WISE, Administrative Judge of the District Court of Urbania County.

For trial on

_____ , 19 ___   *E. Victor Quick*
                                             _____
                                                  Chief Constable

---

RENT NOTICE

DISTRICT COURT OF ANYSTATE FOR THE COUNTY OF URBANIA

Whereas _____ , Lessor by _____ .
his duly qualified Agent or Attorney, has this day filed his written complaint in this court,
praying to have again and repossess the premises in said city known as

No. _____ street
rented from him by _____ , Tenant
alleging there is rent due and unpaid to said Lessor the sum of
_____ dollars, _____ cents.

And that by warrant Lessor may have and again repossess the said premises, together with
judgement for the amount of rent due and costs. Wherefore you are hereby ordered to forth-
with summon and notify said tenant to personally appear before JUSTIN WISE, Administrative Judge of the District Court of Urbania County.

For trial on

_____ , 19 ___   *E. Victor Quick*
                                             _____
                                                  Chief Constable

SCORE SHEET - PART I

TENANTS' POINTS

Round

1   _____   _____   _____   _____   _____   _____

2   _____   _____   _____   _____   _____   _____

3   _____   _____   _____   _____   _____   _____

4   _____   _____   _____   _____   _____   _____

5   _____   _____   _____   _____   _____   _____

6   _____   _____   _____   _____   _____   _____

Total   _____   _____   _____   _____   _____   _____

LANDLORDS' DEBTS

_____   _____   _____   _____

_____   _____   _____   _____

_____   _____   _____   _____

_____   _____   _____   _____

_____   _____   _____   _____

_____   _____   _____   _____

_____   _____   _____   _____

SCORE SHEET - PART II

TENANTS

Total points	___	___	___	___	___
+ Cash on hand	+ ___	+ ___	+ ___	+ ___	+ ___
= Unadjusted score	= ___	= ___	= ___	= ___	= ___
Wear and tear points*	___	___	___	___	___
× 10	× 10 ___	× 10 ___	× 10 ___	× 10 ___	× 10 ___
= Adjustment	= ___	= ___	= ___	= ___	= ___
Unadjusted score	___	___	___	___	___
– Adjustment	– ___	– ___	– ___	– ___	– ___
= Actual score	= ___	= ___	= ___	= ___	= ___

*This includes points from Vacancy and House-empty cards.

LANDLORDS

Cash on hand	___	___	___	___	___
– Total debts	– ___	– ___	– ___	– ___	– ___
= Unadjusted score	= ___	= ___	= ___	= ___	= ___
– Wear and tear costs**	– ___	– ___	– ___	– ___	– ___
= Actual score	= ___	= ___	= ___	= ___	= ___

**This includes costs from Vacancy and House-empty cards, but not City-inspection cards. Remember to check upper right corner of Wear-and-tear cards.

SCORE SHEET - PART I

TENANTS' POINTS

Round

1   _____   _____   _____   _____   _____   _____

2   _____   _____   _____   _____   _____   _____

3   _____   _____   _____   _____   _____   _____

4   _____   _____   _____   _____   _____   _____

5   _____   _____   _____   _____   _____   _____

6   _____   _____   _____   _____   _____   _____

Total   _____   _____   _____   _____   _____   _____

LANDLORDS' DEBTS

_____   _____   _____   _____

_____   _____   _____   _____

_____   _____   _____   _____

_____   _____   _____   _____

_____   _____   _____   _____

_____   _____   _____   _____

_____   _____   _____   _____

SCORE SHEET - PART II

TENANTS

	Total points
+	Cash on hand
=	Unadjusted score
	Wear and tear points*
× 10	
=	Adjustment

	Unadjusted score
−	Adjustment
=	Actual score

*This includes points from Vacancy and House-empty cards.

LANDLORDS

	Cash on hand
−	Total debts
=	Unadjusted score
−	Wear and tear costs**
=	Actual score

**This includes costs from Vacancy and House-empty cards, but not City-inspection cards. Remember to check upper right corner of Wear-and-tear cards.

TENANT

Mrs. Washington—family of 7

Source of income: works as cleaning woman.

TENANT

Mrs. Grant—family of 6

Source of income: husband's Army allotment and part-time work doing laundry and ironing.

TENANT

Mr. & Mrs. Hayes—family of 8

Source of income: Mr. Hayes works in a warehouse.

TENANT

Mrs. Adams—family of 7

Source of income: AFDC (welfare).

TENANT

Mr. & Mrs. Jackson—family of 10

Source of income: Mr. Jackson is a factory worker.

TENANT

Mr. & Mrs. Pierce—family of 2

Source of income: pension, Social Security.

$\frac{1}{2}$

Paint splattered on walls.
Cost of repairs: $80.

Tenant loses 10 points each month.

$\frac{1}{2}$

Paint splattered on walls.
Cost of repairs: $110.

Tenant loses 10 points each month.

$\frac{1}{2}$

Broken windows.
Cost of repairs: $10.

Tenant loses 3 points each month.

$\frac{1}{2}$

Several broken windows.
Cost of repairs: $16.

Tenant loses 5 points each month.

$\frac{1}{2}$

Several windows and one ceiling light fixture broken.
Cost of repairs: $30.

Tenant loses 10 points each month.

No damage.

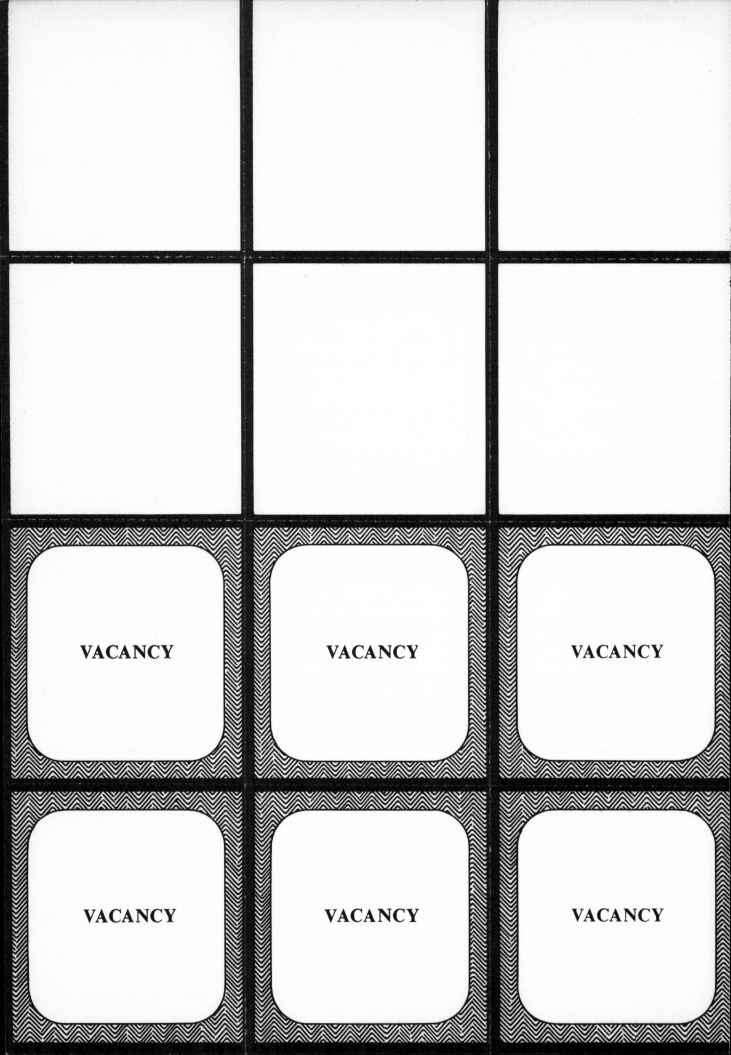

Broken windows.

Cost of repairs: $16.

Tenant loses 5 points each month.

$\frac{1}{2}$

Broken windows.

Cost of repairs: $10.

Tenant loses 3 points each month.

$\frac{1}{2}$

Several broken windows and one broken window sash.

Cost of repairs: $66.

Tenant loses 8 points each month.

$\frac{1}{2}$

All windows broken.
Back door smashed in.
Holes in walls.
Light fixtures broken.
Plumbing fixtures and water pipes stolen.

Cost of repairs: $450.

Tenants lose 40 points per month.

Several windows broken.
Floorboards torn up.
Light fixtures, plumbing, fixtures, and water pipes stolen.

Cost of repairs: $400.

Tenants lose 50 points per month.

All windows broken.
One broken window sash.
Paint spattered on walls.
Floorboards torn up.
Light fixtures broken.
Plumbing fixtures and water pipes stolen.

Cost of repairs: $540.

Tenants lose 40 points per month.

All windows broken.
One broken window sash.
Holes in walls.
Light fixtures broken.
Plumbing fixtures and water pipes stolen.

Cost of repairs: $480.

Tenants lose 50 points per month.

Several windows broken.
Floorboards torn up.
Light fixtures, plumbing fixtures, and water pipes stolen.

Cost of repairs: $400.

Tenants lose 50 points per month.

Several windows broken.
Back door lock broken.
Paint splattered on walls.
Light fixtures broken.
Plumbing fixtures and water pipes stolen.

Cost of repairs: $420.

Tenants lose 40 points per month.

All windows broken.
Back door smashed in.
Holes in walls.
Light fixtures broken.
Plumbing fixtures and water pipes stolen.

Cost of repairs: $450.

Tenants lose 40 points per month.

Several windows broken.
Floorboards torn up.
Light fixtures, plumbing fixtures, and water pipes stolen.

Cost of repairs: $400.

Tenants lose 50 points per month.

All windows broken.
One broken window sash.
Paint spattered on walls.
Floorboards torn up.
Light fixtures broken.
Plumbing fixtures and water pipes stolen.

Cost of repairs: $540.

Tenants lose 40 points per month.

VACANCY

VACANCY

VACANCY

HOUSE
EMPTY

HOUSE
EMPTY

HOUSE
EMPTY

HOUSE
EMPTY

HOUSE
EMPTY

HOUSE
EMPTY

HOUSE
EMPTY

HOUSE
EMPTY

HOUSE
EMPTY

All windows broken.
One broken window sash.
Holes in walls.
Light fixtures broken.
Plumbing fixtures and water pipes stolen.

Cost of repairs: $480.

Tenants lose 50 points per month.

Several windows broken.
Floorboards torn up.
Light fixtures, plumbing fixtures, and water pipes stolen.

Cost of repairs: $400.

Tenants lose 50 points per month.

Several windows broken.
Back door lock broken.
Paint splattered on walls.
Light fixtures broken.
Plumbing fixtures and water pipes stolen.

Cost of repairs: $420.

Tenants lose 40 points per month.

Broken water heater.

Cost of replacement: $110.

Both tenants lose 15 points each month this condition is not corrected.

2

Tenants without children: No problems

Tenants with children: Sink drain clogged.

Cost of repairs: $10.

Tenant loses 15 points each month this condition is not corrected

---

No problems.

$\frac{1}{2}$

Trash in backyard.

Cost of removal: $12.

Both tenants lose 10 points each month this condition is not corrected.

$\frac{1}{2}$

Clogged bathtub drain.

Cost of repairs: $10.

Tenant loses 15 points each month this condition is not corrected.

$\frac{1}{2}$

Trash in backyard.

Cost of removal: $16.

Both tenants lose 10 points each month this condition is not corrected.

$\frac{1}{2}$

Tenants without children: No problems.

Tenants with children: Broken window.

Cost of repairs: $6.

Tenant loses 2 points each month this condition is not corrected.

Outside back stairs rickety and unsafe.

Cost of repairs: $30.

Tenant on upper floor loses 10 points each month this condition is not corrected.

$\frac{1}{2}$

Paint cracked and peeling.

Cost of repainting: $110.

Tenant loses 5 points each month this condition is not corrected.

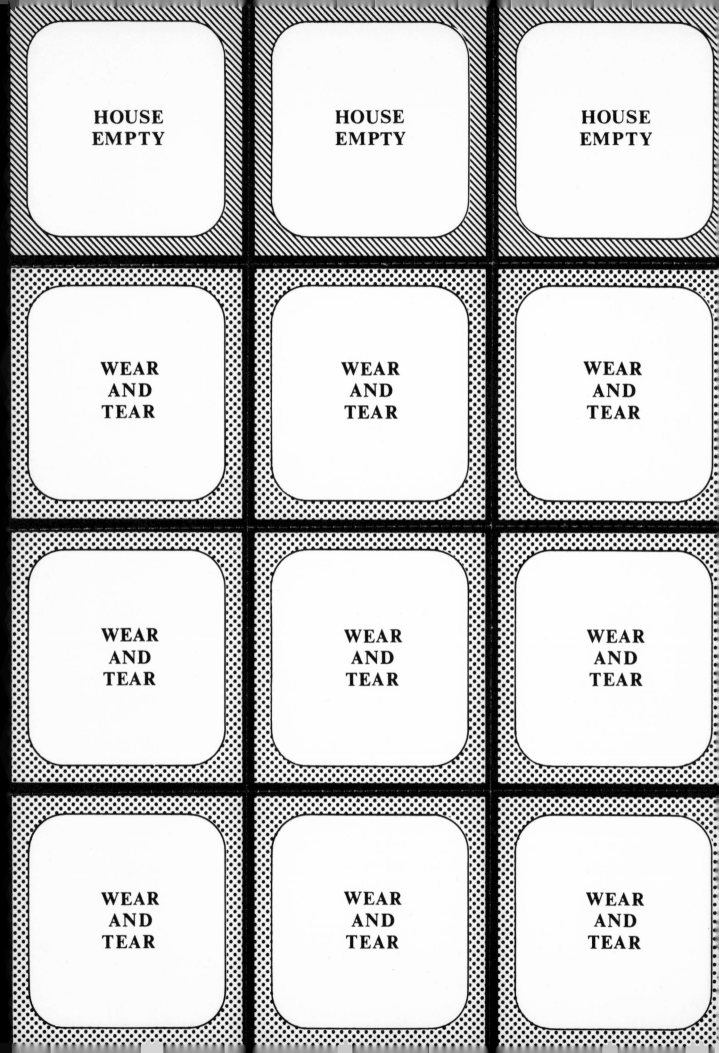

2

Tenants without children: No problems.

Tenants with children: Clogged toilet drain.

Cost of repairs: $25.

Tenant loses 25 points each month this condition is not corrected.

No problems.

Hole in living-room floor.

Cost of repairs: $25.

Tenant loses 10 points each month this condition is not corrected.

Paint peeling in two rooms.

Cost of repainting: $60.

Tenant loses 5 points each month this condition is not corrected.

$\frac{1}{2}$

Trash in backyard.

Cost of removal: $16.

Both tenants lose 10 points each month this condition is not corrected.

No problems.

$\frac{1}{2}$

Tenants without children: No problems.

Tenants with children: Broken ceiling light fixtures.

Cost of replacement: $20.

Tenant loses 5 points each month this condition is not corrected.

Plaster falling from ceiling.

Cost of repairs: $25.

Tenant loses 5 points each month this condition is not corrected.

$\frac{1}{2}$

Paint peeling and plaster crumbling in one room.

Cost of repairs: $40.

Tenant loses 5 points each month this condition is not corrected.

No problems.

2

Leaking toilet tank.

Cost of repairs: $40.

Tenant loses 15 points each month this condition is not corrected.

Loose floor boards.

Cost of repairs: $15.

Tenant loses 5 points each month this condition is not corrected.

Paint cracked and peeling.

Cost of repainting: $140.

Tenant loses 5 points each month this condition is not corrected.

$\frac{1}{2}$

No problems.

Tenants without children: No problems.

Tenants with children: Broken window panes.

Cost of repairs: $10.

Tenant loses 5 points each month this condition is not corrected.

$\frac{1}{2}$

Tenants without children: No problems.

Tenants with children: Large dent in living room wall–board.

Cost of repairs: $30.

Tenant loses 2 points each month this condition is not corrected.

$\frac{1}{2}$

Severe roach infestation.

Cost of extermination: $40.

Both tenants lose 15 points each month this condition is not corrected.

This card applies to both apartments.

$\frac{1}{2}$

Tenants without children: No problems.

Tenants with children: Broken window panes and sash.

Cost of repairs: $50.

Tenant loses 5 points each month this condition is not corrected.

$\frac{1}{2}$

Front-door lock will not engage.

Cost of repairs: $15.

Tenant loses 25 points each month this condition is not corrected.

This card applies to both apartments.

Trash cans dented and rusty.

Cost of replacement: $10.

Tenant loses 2 points each month this condition is not corrected.

This card applies to both apartments.

$\frac{1}{2}$

Light switch broken.

Cost of repairs: $10.

Tenant loses 5 points each month this condition is not repaired.

Exterior paint is cracked and peeling.

Cost of repainting: $80.

Tenant loses 2 points each month this condition is not corrected.

This card applies to both apartments.

$\frac{1}{2}$

Roof leaks.

Cost of repairs: $50,

Tenant on upper floor loses 15 points each month this condition is not corrected, no matter which tenant drew this card.

2

Roof leaks.

Cost of repairs: $40.

Tenant on upper floor loses 15 points each month this condition is not corrected, no matter which tenant drew this card.

2

WEAR
AND
TEAR

WEAR
AND
TEAR

WEAR
AND
TEAR

WEAR
AND
TEAR

WEAR
AND
TEAR

WEAR
AND
TEAR

WEAR
AND
TEAR

WEAR
AND
TEAR

WEAR
AND
TEAR

WEAR
AND
TEAR

WEAR
AND
TEAR

WEAR
AND
TEAR

No problems.

2

Tenants without children: No problems.

Tenants with children: Clogged toilet drain.

Cost of repairs: $25.

Tenant loses 25 points each month this condition is not corrected.

$\frac{1}{2}$

Tenants without children: No problems.

Tenants with children: Broken ceiling light fixtures.

Cost of replacement: $20.

Tenant loses 5 points each month this condition is not corrected.

$\frac{1}{2}$

2 additional violations.

Cost of repairs: $20.

$\frac{1}{2}$

6 additional violations.

Cost of repairs: $65.

$\frac{1}{2}$

7 additional violations.

Cost of repairs: $150

$\frac{1}{2}$

9 additional violations.

Cost of repairs: $160.

$\frac{1}{2}$

3 additional violations.

Cost of repairs: $50.

$\frac{1}{2}$

2 additional violations.

Cost of repairs: $30.

$\frac{1}{2}$

11 additional violations.

Cost of repairs: $135.

$\frac{1}{2}$

5 additional violations.

Cost of repairs: $60.

$\frac{1}{2}$

4 additional violations.

Cost of repairs: $80.

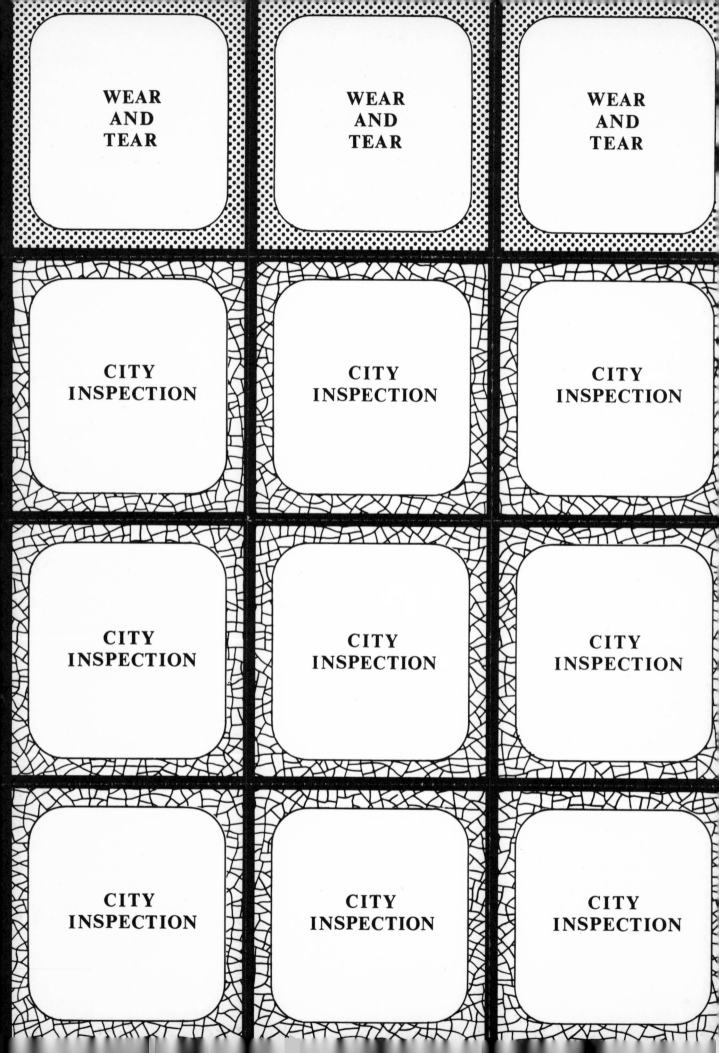

WEAR
AND
TEAR

WEAR
AND
TEAR

WEAR
AND
TEAR

CITY
INSPECTION

CITY
INSPECTION

CITY
INSPECTION

CITY
INSPECTION

CITY
INSPECTION

CITY
INSPECTION

CITY
INSPECTION

CITY
INSPECTION

CITY
INSPECTION

$\frac{1}{2}$

8 additional violations.

Cost of repairs: $125.

Purse-snatching. Lose $30.

If you have children—your youngest child is sick. Pay medical expenses of $40, unless you receive AFDC or an Army allotment.

If you have children—one of your children is hit by a car. Pay medical expenses of $35, unless you receive AFDC or an Army allotment.

If you have a full-time job—you are laid off for one week. Receive only three fourths of your regular income.

If you have children, pay extra clothing expenses of $15.

Armed robbery. Lose $15.

Armed robbery. Lose $25.

Purse-snatching. Lose $20.

If you have children, pay extra clothing expenses of $20.

Broken eyeglasses. Pay $25 unless you receive AFDC or an Army allotment.

If you have a full-time job—overtime work brings you an extra $25.

CHANCE

CHANCE

CITY
INSPECTION

CHANCE

CHANCE

CHANCE

CHANCE

CHANCE

CHANCE

CHANCE

CHANCE

CHANCE

Receive income and pay expenses as usual.

Receive income and pay expenses as usual.

Receive income and pay expenses as usual.

Receive income and pay expenses as usual.

Receive income and pay expenses as usual.

Receive income and pay expenses as usual.

Receive income and pay expenses as usual.

Receive income and pay expenses as usual.

Receive income and pay expenses as usual.

Receive income and pay expenses as usual.

Receive income and pay expenses as usual.

Receive income and pay expenses as usual.

Receive income and pay expenses as usual.

Receive income and pay expenses as usual.

Receive income and pay expenses as usual.

Receive income and pay expenses as usual.

Receive income and pay expenses as usual.

Receive income and pay expenses as usual.

Receive income and pay expenses as usual.

Receive income and pay expenses as usual.

Receive income and pay expenses as usual.

Receive income and pay expenses as usual.

Receive income and pay expenses as usual.

Receive income and pay expenses as usual.